T0079832

SMART MACHINES
AND SERVICE WORK

FIELD NOTES

SERIES EDITOR: Paul Mattick

A series of books providing in-depth analyses of today's global turmoil as it unfolds. Each book focuses on an important feature of our present-day economic, political and cultural condition, addressing local and international issues. Field Notes examines the many dimensions of today's social predicament and provides a radical, politically and critically engaged voice to global debates.

Published in association with the *Brooklyn Rail*

Titles in the series:

A Happy Future is a Thing of the Past: The Greek Crisis and Other Disasters
PAVLOS ROUFOS

Hinterland: America's New Landscape of Class and Conflict
PHIL A. NEEL

No Home for You Here: A Memoir of Class and Culture
ADAM THERON-LEE RENSCH

Smart Machines and Service Work: Automation in an Age of Stagnation
JASON E. SMITH

SMART MACHINES AND SERVICE WORK

Automation in an Age of Stagnation

JASON E. SMITH

REAKTION BOOKS

Published by Reaktion Books Ltd
Unit 32, Waterside
44–48 Wharf Road
London N1 7UX, UK
www.reaktionbooks.co.uk

Printed and bound in Great Britain by TJ Press, Padstow, Cornwall

A catalogue record for this book is available from the British Library

ISBN 978 1 78914 318 8

Contents

Automation 2.0

"Rise of the Robots," the "Second Machine Age," a "World without Work": these are the catchphrases coined over the past decade to characterize the current epoch of self-driving cars and smart cities, of Twitter bots, deep fakes, and mass surveillance. Indeed, over the last ten years, the texture of everyday life has been rent and reshaped by technological breakthroughs in the spheres of leisure, sociality, and politics. Shopping, friendship, and elections will never be the same. As extensive as these changes have been, the loudest voices heralding a new age of automation claim that these transformations are the outward signs of a more profound social transformation that is already underway. Hailing primarily from Silicon Valley and MBA programs, but sometimes op-ed pages and presidential primaries, these commentators claim that a new breed of smart machines have begun to revolutionize the core productive capacity of the world's advanced economies, drawing them out of their decades-long stupor. When the "brilliant technologies" of the twenty-first century are fully implemented in restaurants and doctors' offices, schools and hotels, the ailing and listless leaders of the global economy—in North America, Europe, and East Asia—will find new life, we're told, as a new age of prodigious wealth creation dawns. A salient feature of this prospective revitalization will be an explosion in labor productivity, as fewer and fewer workers turn out more and more goods and services. What will people *do*, these same prognosticators ask, in the coming decades, when up to half the currently existing jobs in America are lost to these wondrous machines? The world of smart cars, cities, homes, and hospitals might also be a world of joblessness, want, and misery for many or even most.

In the pages that follow, I scrutinize these claims closely, asking what presumptions they are founded on, and what conclusions they assume. Discourses on automation today take for granted the resumption of a prior pattern of mid-twentieth-century automation that may no longer apply. The term itself was coined in 1946 by a Ford vice president, in an era when the industries producing steel, automobiles, and petroleum by-products introduced computer-assisted labor-saving technologies. Factories that had been roiled by worker unrest were expanding production at unprecedented rates, and with far fewer workers. With these dramatic changes came a surfeit of studies, reports, warnings, and enthusiasms regarding automation. The topic was momentous enough to warrant Senate Hearings in 1955, and in 1964 Lyndon Johnson created a National Commission on Technology, Automation, and Economic Progress. The academic discipline of industrial sociology flourished as it tracked the changes in the nature of work and class composition induced by the cybernetic revolution in industry. At the same time, the decades after the war were a golden age for the labor movement: the rising productivity of workers in industry created the material conditions for winning substantial gains in wages, while union leaders increasingly collaborated with business owners in the management of large firms. These successes, however, were shadowed by the livelihoods lost to the very surge in productivity that made these gains possible. As workforces in heavy industry were trimmed, many found employment in the growing service sector, which began to swell in the 1960s, as workers displaced from capital-intensive industries were absorbed into sectors such as education and healthcare, government and finance, restaurants, retail, and "business services." But some, and in particular, black workers, were less "fortunate." As union militant and theorist James Boggs wrote in 1964, if black workers could once leave tenant farms and Jim Crow to find work in factories, now the "the displaced men have nowhere to go."[1]

Today, we are told, it is no longer the manufacturing sector that will be subject to huge changes due to labor-saving technologies. What is being transformed now is the vast service sector. The same jobs that proliferated in the wake of automation's first wave will in their turn be replaced en masse in this new wave. Call it Automation 2.0. But if the first wave of automation took place in a postwar boom, current conversations about coming disruptions to the labor market are occurring in the midst of severe and ongoing economic stagnation. In fact, since the early 1970s, the world's advanced economies have experienced slowdowns in almost all key categories and especially in GDP and labor productivity growth. The result has been a decades-long flatlining of wage-earners' purchasing power. The pattern has been particularly acute since 2008, with the onset of the Great Recession. Real wages for most workers fell while unemployment soared, business investment collapsed, and rates of labor productivity growth in some cases declined for the first time in almost a century. According to a 2018 Bank of England report, "average productivity growth" for the ten-year period beginning in 2008 produced "the worst decade since the late 18th century."[2]

Why, given these exceptionally bleak conditions, has the past decade given rise to such a flurry of debate around automation? In late 2007, as the U.S. subprime mortgage market was collapsing and big investment banks began to go under, the once-beleaguered U.S. home computer manufacturer Apple released its first iPhone, an event that would revolutionize the field of consumer electronics. The arrival of this device was soon followed by the sudden prominence of social media platforms like Facebook and Google, and e-commerce giants such as Amazon and Alibaba. In *Smart Machines and Service Work*, I argue that the ubiquity of these devices—smartphones that integrate telecommunications, shopping, streaming video, and sociality in a single gadget— and platforms in the everyday life of their users, combined with the central role the so-called "tech" companies came to play in the stock market bubble of the post-crisis decade, provides an important context for understanding the concurrent and urgent debates around automation. However thoroughgoing the effects these machines and networks have had on the experiences of shopping, cultural consumption, navigating cities, or financial speculation, they have had negligible effects on one key economic variable: labor productivity in the workplace.

Back in 1987, Robert Solow observed that "you can see the computer age everywhere but in the productivity statistics."[3] This curious fact—the proliferation of computing technology and digital networks alongside increasingly sluggish productivity growth rates—came to be known as the "productivity paradox." For years, economists have struggled to explain it, either by arguing that the nature of the technologies involved makes it hard to measure productivity advances already taking place, or by proposing the existence of a "lag" in the diffusion of all-purpose technologies such as steam engines, electrical grids, and automation across diverse workplaces and entire economies. Today's automation enthusiasts and theorists continue to make these arguments, with the most sophisticated accounts mapping these delayed effects onto theories of technological change that posit long-wave patterns of economic expansion and contraction unfolding over 25- and 50-year cycles. Yet even those who construct these models have begun to acknowledge that these delays in diffusion have been drawn out long enough—Intel produced the first silicon microchip in 1970—to compromise their explanatory power. Another approach is required.

The argument I make in *Smart Machines and Service Work* takes a different tack altogether. I make the case that there are three primary reasons for the relatively insignificant impact new forms of automation are having on labor productivity growth rates in the world's advanced economies. First, the types of labor processes many automation theorists suggest are vulnerable to replacement by smart machines in fact require an intuitive, embodied, and socially mediated form of knowledge or skill that even the most advanced machine-learning programs cannot master. This is especially the case with so-called "personal services," the fastest-growing segment of today's job market. These activities require in-person interactions between providers and consumers that pose technological, moral, and even legal limits to their replacement by machines. These limits are, I contend, reinforced by an even more powerful disincentive to automate certain lines of production: the prevalence of cheap labor in the advanced economies. When workers will take jobs that are poorly paid because nothing else is available, there is little reason for business owners to invest in expensive and soon obsolete machinery to do their work. In the pages that follow, I show that this prevalence of cheap labor, indexed by decades of stagnant wages for workers, is itself an effect of technological stagnation. Wage gains for workers depend primarily on prior gains in labor productivity, which in turn require elevated rates of business investment to develop and implement ever-newer technologies that will continually reshape labor processes. As I demonstrate in detail in Chapter Five, however, the u.s. economy since 1980 has demonstrated a steady decline in private-sector investment; since 2000, the downward trend has accelerated dramatically. This collapse in investment, occurring against the background of the rise of the tech giants, points to a still more profound disorder at the core of the advanced capitalist economies of North America, Europe, and Japan: a crisis of profitability whose roots lie in a decades-long expansion of what I call, following the classical political economists, "unproductive" labor.

The recent and sudden onset of the COVID-19 pandemic (I write this in late May 2020) and, with it, the government-imposed shutdowns of the economies of Europe and North America, has unexpectedly revived interest in the ongoing debates surrounding automation. Many who have advocated for or simply described the inevitability of the large-scale automation of key sectors of these economies have seized the moment, while adopting a new rhetorical tack. It is now claimed that those workers deemed— but by whom?—"essential" might now profit from the use of robots to carry out many of the most dangerous tasks required of "frontline" workers during the crisis. Warehouse workers, grocery store clerks, hospital staff, and delivery drivers might, it is argued, be kept safe from exposure to the deadly virus if automated devices are deployed to perform these tasks in their place. Such protections, however, would most likely be paid for with a loss of income, throwing these same workers back onto the labor market in search of work. There, other occupations, whose tasks are less likely to be performed by machines, might absorb those "lucky" enough to find work at all.

We should remain circumspect, in any case, when considering the possibilities that businesses would invest in automated machinery in the interest of ensuring worker safety. Such largesse is not often demonstrated by those who employ wage labor in order to generate their own incomes. Other arguments, less naive but equally implausible, have surfaced as well. A report published in the early phase of the shutdown contended that, historically, businesses that have managed to survive economic crises are compelled to make significant changes to their production processes during them. The Brookings Institute argues that

> Robots' infiltration of the workforce doesn't occur at
> a steady, gradual pace. Instead, automation happens in
> bursts, concentrated especially in bad times such as in
> the wake of economic shocks, when humans become

relatively more expensive as firms' revenues rapidly decline. At these moments, employers shed less-skilled workers and replace them with technology and higher-skilled workers, which increases labor productivity as a recession tapers off.[4]

No one will dispute the contention that workers become more expensive when their output drops off in the midst of a crisis, or that less-skilled workers will be the first laid off as a result. Should these workers be replaced by machines, some would likely be employed elsewhere in the economy, building and maintaining these machines. But in many cases, the machines that would be deployed would not entirely replace workers. The robots currently being used in "essential" sectors, such as the decontamination robots introduced into hospitals, do not replace workers so much as force them to learn new tasks: these are not autonomous robots, and must be guided remotely by human hands. In the case of online shopping, the spike in traffic on sites like Amazon.com and Walmart.com during the pandemic has in fact triggered a burst in demand for cheap, human labor, either to meet a labor shortfall in warehouses or, in the final segment of the retail chain, to deliver goods directly to consumer households. Amazon, for example, recently announced it was hiring 100,000 new workers for the warehouse operations and delivery services; Instacart, a grocery delivery service few had heard of before the crisis, has taken on a staggering 550,000 new "shoppers" in less than two months.[5]

Above all, we should not anticipate, as Brookings does, a surge in automation in a period during which "firms' revenues rapidly decline," especially in a situation in which up to 40 percent of the u.s. labor force is out of work. In a context in which business revenue has collapsed—in many sectors, it disappeared almost entirely, overnight—it is hard to fathom where the resources to fund a new round of fixed capital expenditures will be found; those few companies with cash on hand are likely to undertake another round of stock buybacks, as they did over the past decade, rather than contemplating the less lucrative prospect of investing in plant and equipment. In a context in which mass unemployment will mean tens of millions of people, desperate for income, will take any work, however dangerous, at reduced wages, any uptick in business spending will most likely take advantage of the prevailing low wages. For the most part, however, companies are likely to reduce their payrolls dramatically and, without changing the way they produce goods and services, force incremental upticks in productivity by intensifying the labor of those who remain employed, and who labor under the threat of further job losses and pay cuts. It is unlikely, then, that the coronavirus shutdowns will spell the end of our age of stagnation; to the contrary, they are sure to prolong it indefinitely, or at least until workers themselves, employed or unemployed, act to forcefully bring about its end.

The current drift of the "automation" economy, with its rapidly swelling low-skill, low-wage labor market, poses special obstacles to organization and action for an increasingly frag-mented workforce. The rise of the "servant economy," I argue, increasingly forces workers into smaller, spatially dispersed workplaces, where they carry out labor-intensive production processes that, because they rely on putatively innate (and therefore "gendered") social and interpersonal knowledges and behaviors, are deemed low-skill occupations and are therefore poorly paid. And yet, the past ten years have seen a remarkable (if still modest) upsurge in worker combativity, whether in public sector strikes in education, or in mass movements outside work-places altogether, like the Occupy movement in the u.s., or the recent *gilets jaunes* upheaval in France. *Smart Machines and Service Work* therefore concludes by asking why today's environment of economic stagnation and crisis has given rise to this combination of "classic" struggles in the workplace and newer forms of conflict in the streets.

one

A Little History of Automation

N o one word captures the direction and dilemma of the current moment—the post-2008 crisis period—quite like *automation.* It is invoked time and again in the dailies, the business press, and dinner-table conversation as an imminent possibility of the present: a poorly defined word and idea that carries an ambivalent charge, both awe and anxiety. Since the onset of the global economic crisis of 2008, the sudden renewal of interest in the allure of automation has picked up where the discourse of the postwar period left off, though now the rhetoric has become especially breathless. A day does not pass when we are not greeted with news of an insurrectionary "rise" of the robots (originating in the 1920s, this term is derived from the Czech *robota*, meaning "forced labor"), or regaled with stories of such neighboring developments in information technology as "big data," "algorithms," or "artificial intelligence." These latter phenomena often receive their own enthusiastic treatment, but they are better understood as aspects or component parts of a more sweeping mutation that is at once pointed out and passed over with the blanket term *automation.* These terms all are made to drift into metaphysical terrain at times, as fascinated witnesses put them through science-fictional paces; at stake, in these reveries, are the definition and nature of thought, of ethical responsibility, of the human itself. The more secular uses of these terms, however, gravitate around the day-in, day-out preoccupations of workers in the wealthiest nations on earth. Few doubt that automation and its forces are gathering just around the corner. Many envision these forces as an army with irresistible culling power, come to harvest and take away tens of millions of jobs and livelihoods.

The current wave of wonder and fear mounting over the prospect of large-scale automation and its purportedly devastating potential effects on the labor markets of the OECD countries can be dated to around 2013 or so, at a moment when the U.S. economy was still wading through the high waters of the crisis—in January 2013, the official unemployment rate was 8 percent—and Europe was suffering the worst of its ongoing public debt fiasco. Erik Brynjolfsson and Andrew McAfee's 2011 book, *Race against the Machine*, anticipated and abetted this trend; their follow-up, 2014's *The Second Machine Age*, is its fullest expression. In the midst of unusual and sustained jobless rates in the U.S., the *New York Times* and other prominent publications have cultivated a subgenre of timely articles—features and editorials—with hand-wringing titles like "Will Robots Take Our Children's Jobs?" and "The Long-term Jobs Killer Is Not China. It's Automation." *The Economist*, often more measured in its assessment of the trend, billed its special report on automation with an especially splashy title: "Automation and Anxiety. Will Smarter Machines Cause Mass Unemployment?" While a not-negligible minority of voices in the debates around automation remain circumspect in the face of claims about a looming wholesale replacement of workers by machines, such scruples are often buried at the bottom of the page, and rarely merit a bold headline of their own. The prevailing sentiment in the business papers, in tech circles, and in the popular discourse around "the second machine age" is what has, ambivalently, been termed "optimism": the belief or calculated wager that *this time it's different*, and that the technological change currently underway is irreversible, and will ravage and restructure the world of work from top to bottom.

A recent opinion piece in the *New York Times* making the case for a federal jobs guarantee is typical in this regard. Written by a labor historian whose training and expertise should encourage caution in these matters, the editorial opens with the observation that almost half of currently existing occupations in the state of Ohio are "at risk of automation," a defining if poorly defined catchphrase of the past decade.[1] The op-ed is content to let the threat loom over its readers; rather than worrying over the evidence or argumentation for this dire conclusion (the scholar in question cites no less an authority than the *Columbus Dispatch*), it moves quickly to a solution, pushing a policy—a 1970s-era federal jobs guarantee—currently being floated by a number of Democratic Party presidential aspirants edging leftward as the U.S. political weather shifts. Peter Frase's 2016 short book *Four Futures: Life after Capitalism* is more forthright about its intentions. An inventive exercise in imagining the social effects of near-full automation, *Four Futures* throws up its hands without even entering the debate around the prospects and effects of a coming wave of automation; it instead "takes for granted the premise of the automation optimists, that within as little as a few decades we could live in a *Star Trek*-like world where . . . a large amount of the labor currently done by humans is in the process of being automated away."[2] Like many commentators on the subject of automation, our labor historian and our socialist futurist equally and uncritically rely on a single 2013 study put out by Oxford University's Martin School predicting that some 47 percent of U.S. jobs are "at risk" of automation.[3] Other studies pile on with even more dramatic prognostications, raising the bar closer to 80 percent in the not-too-distant future.[4] These accounts, which are shared by a wide range of commentators whatever their political orientation or ambition, rely on a single unexamined assumption: that the sector in which nearly all new job creation over the past quarter-century has taken place—the service sector—will soon be decimated by a legion of "intelligent" machines. As will become apparent below, claims like these are almost always made with little consideration for the construction and viability of the category of services to begin with, or what macroeconomic and social pressures, let alone technological obstacles, would compel or prevent the eventual replacement of this entire "sector" by robots, able to serve beers, accept payments, and care for young children, the sick, and the old.

Despite the new discourse on automation's conviction that this time it's different, the history of human civilization abounds in tales of automata; so much so, that human civilization and the dream and fear of automation are hard to tell apart. For much of that history, these strange devices remained mere notions, conceived in a weave of myth and fantasy. In his *The Philosophy of Manufactures* of 1835, in which he describes and advocates at length for what he calls "the automatic factory" or "the automatic plan," the Scottish writer Andrew Ure compiles a little history of automata dating as far back as the statues of Memnon, which he speculates emitted sounds when struck by sunlight, by means of "concealed organ-pipes"; he does so in order to distinguish these deceptive devices from those employed in the self-moving machine complexes of the textile industry.[5] What set the often ingenious mechanisms of the past apart from the enormous apparatuses deployed in English workshops was their aesthetic vocation, the fact that they were devised "chiefly for public amusement or mystification, without any object of utility." Such "self-acting machines," Ure concludes, "however admirable as exercises of mechanical science, do nothing towards the supply of the physical necessities of society." While in his own era they were composed primarily for "public amusement," historically they were often fabricated for the private delight of the idle rich, whether in the courts of Chinese, Muslim, or European royalty, or on the estates of the landed nobility. Until the nineteenth century, such "curious contrivances" were only proposed "to the purposes of luxury." It required the consolidation of the industrialist class in Manchester and the owners of the Lancashire cotton mills to put these "automatic inventions" in the service of the laboring population as a whole, applying them "to the production of food and domestic accommodation."[6]

Where does the iconic technological artifact of our own crisis decade—the Apple iPhone, first offered to the u.s. public in June 2007, on the very eve of the economic meltdown—fit into such a drawn-out historical narrative? Can the smartphone, so revolutionary in its shaping of middle-class American behavior (driving, shopping, "communicating"), be assimilated to those technological inventions Ure describes as meeting the "physical necessities of society"? Or does this device have its place, instead, among the vast array of gadgets or toys thrown up by this history, whose purpose is "chiefly for public amusement or mystification"?

Automata appear in the cultural record of Europe as early as Homer's *Iliad*, where the god of the forge, Hephaestus, is depicted assembling self-moving "tripods" that would serve the gods food and drink in the banquet halls of Olympus. In his *Politics*, Aristotle imagines for a moment a world in which the slave labor so prevalent in classical and democratic Greece would be replaced by *automata*, only in order to argue that because slavery is an "ethical" relation and not an economic one, such labor-saving machinery would by no means obviate the need for such an institution.[7] In the early modern period, at a moment when the feudal organization of social production had yet to complete its decomposition, and when new social forces and relations had yet to fully emerge, the figure of the automaton began to assume a special place in the European cultural imaginary. It is then that the European languages begin first to find use for the Greek terms *autómaton* and *automata*. In the writings of Rabelais, for example, we encounter one of the earliest occurrences of the word, when in Chapter 24 of *Gargantua* he pauses to marvel over "several little automatic machines, that is, that moved by themselves."[8]

A little over a century later, in his Second Meditation, Descartes will glance up from his piece of wax, in the midst of a celebrated demonstration regarding how we can know extended bodies only through inspection of the mind rather than through the perception of the senses, to note that those same senses cannot determine whether or not the men he sees through the window are "ghosts or feigned men moved only by springs." Still later, in his *Monadology* (1714), the philosopher Leibniz will characterize the "monads"—his name for the simple or created substances—of his treatise's title as being "so to speak incorporeal Automata," impervious to any causal influence from other monads, and therefore the "source of their own inner actions."

Such literary and philosophical appropriations of the figure of the automaton would soon find their match in the vibrant scientific culture of the eighteenth and nineteenth centuries. A notable example can be found in the once celebrated inventions of Jacques de Vaucanson, whose automated flautist and drummer were quickly upstaged by his fully functioning "automatic" duck, which ate, digested, and defecated with a lifelike precision (he also designed a mechanical loom that was never built). Many of these supposedly self-moving devices were feats of deception of one sort or another, an air of the street carnival enveloping them. In a celebrated passage from *The Prelude*, Wordsworth places "the Invisible girl"—a large sphere seemingly able to answer questions posed to it, an early nineteenth-century Siri—alongside "the learned Pig, / The Stone-eater, the man that swallows fire, / Giants, Ventriloquists . . ." More notoriously, there was Maelzel's chess-playing automaton, which toured Europe and the u.s. in the 1830s and which, according to Ure, "imitates very remarkably a living being, endowed with all the resources of intelligence, for executing the combinations of profound study." In fact, the chess-playing "mechanical Turk"—a puppet wearing a stereotypical fez, shirt, and mustache—concealed within its innards a human chess-master, most likely a dwarf small enough to fit into such confines.[9]

Though the Greek noun *autómaton* appears very early in European cultural history, the adjectival form "automatic" did not surface in the modern European languages until the mid-eighteenth century, first in French (*automatique*) and English, a bit later in German (*automatisch*). In contrast to the primary usage of the term "automaton," its field of application was almost exclusively physiology and medicine. "Automatic" was initially used to describe the pulsations of living rather than mechanical processes. Specifically, it referred to those biological or animate processes that occur spontaneously in the body, without the intervention of the will; a central example was the pumping action of the heart and the circulation of blood. It should be remembered, though, that the term arose in a century in which the animal organism was generally considered a machine, a conception that, among scientists and savants, largely prevails today. When Norbert Wiener was developing the theory of cybernetics in the 1940s, he observed that the phenomenon of "feedback" was readily apparent both in biology and engineering. His very definition of cybernetics—"the scientific study of control and communication in the animal and the machine"—makes it clear that the phenomena of self-regulating systems he wanted to isolate cut across the distinction between living and inanimate, animal and machine.

Ford executive Del Harder's first use of the term "automation" in 1946 did not yet mean what it would come to signify over the course of the next decade and a half, or what it has come to mean today. In the years after the Second World War, Harder, a vice president for manufacturing, was tasked with reorganizing Ford's massive River Rouge complex, and had only recently established a secretive automation department within the company. In fact, the automobile industry would not begin to automate significant parts of factories until the mid-1950s, a process that would continue well into the 1960s. By "automation" Harder was not even referring to the newest technological innovations developed, and put to use, in the 1930s and the war that followed; he meant merely the growing preponderance of what he called "electro-mechanical, pneumatic, and hydraulic" devices in factory production. Many of these systems or techniques were initially developed, albeit in primitive versions, in the mid- to late nineteenth century. Moreover, when in 1868 James Clerk Maxwell published his celebrated paper establishing the theoretical basis for the operation of engine governors, the core technological premise—a centrifugal governor that regulated the speed of steam engines—had been in existence for eighty years, having first been patented by James Watt. What Harder called automation referred primarily to the refinement of techniques and principles that had been in place for decades, indeed, for a century or more. Over the next decade, however, automation began to mean more and more the use of recently developed innovation in "feedback" technologies, and the "self-regulation" not only of individual machines, but of entire factories or production sites.

An at times humorous image of the postwar automatic factory was painted by industry insiders like Harder and by enthusiasts in the business press, a picture predicated on the transformation of the dirty, noisy rough-and-tumble of the factory floor, often hosting tens of thousands of workers for eight hours a day, into an antiseptic space resembling a scientific lab. Already in 1835, Harder's lineal ancestor Andrew Ure had described the "automatic factory" as housed in clean, well-lit "spacious halls"—"apartments more airy and salubrious than those of the metropolis in which our legislature and fashionable aristocracies assemble"—within which the assembled workers are relieved of their burdens to such an extent that they are relegated to "mere onlookers of machines."[10] The vision spelled out in a 1946 *Fortune* spread on the automatic factory echoed, in its basic outlines, that proposed by Ure more than a century before: "Imagine, if you will, a factory as clean, spacious and continuously operating as a hydroelectric plant. The production floor is barren of men. Only a few engineers, technicians, and operators walk about a balcony above, before a great wall of master controls, inserting and checking records, watching and adjusting batteries of control instruments."[11] By 1954, a professor of electrical engineering at the Massachusetts Institute of Technology (MIT), and author of an already standard 1948 book on the principles of servomechanisms, offered still another image of the future factory, this time in a speech given to a steelworkers' union: "steel has become an industry wherein I would not think it facetious if the workmen wore tuxedos on the job."[12] Such speculative blueprints for the heavy industry of the coming decades both transformed the shop floor into a pristine, studious workshop in which scientific expertise is valued above all and recast it as a society ball at which drudgery and physical exertion are replaced by a kind of dance, the "workmen" improbably play-acting the leisure rituals of their social superiors. Here, too, the reveries of mid-century industrialists and their *consiglieri* echoed, in dovetailing work and play, the primal propagandist of the workless factory. Ure, describing the work performed by young children in the factories of his day, compared their activity to the concerted movements of organized play: "the work of these lively elves seemed to resemble a sport, in which habit gave them a pleasing dexterity."[13]

In his important mid-1950s examination of the discourse around and prospects for automation in industry, Friedrich Pollock offered his own pithy conceptual definition of automation as a "technique of industrial production [in which] the machines are 'controlled' by machines."[14] Here the emphasis, despite the scare quotes, must be placed directly on the verb "control." In his notebooks for *Capital* dating from the late 1850s, Marx already envisioned the gradual diminution of the role of human labor in the production process. As its physical activity was replaced by self-acting machines, "the human being," he wrote, stands in relation to the production process "more as watchman and regulator," rather than its initiator or primary component. The new automated or "control" technologies first sketched in the 1930s, and implemented for the most part after the war, would replace even this "watchman" who "steps to the side of the production process instead of being its chief actor."[15]

The notion of "control" placed between quotation marks by Pollock has a technical sense as well as a vernacular one. In the wake of the theoretical and scientific breakthroughs of the 1930s, a new territory was opened in the field of engineering: control systems engineering. Control theory deals with the application of the principles of automatic control to dynamic systems; it is concerned with managing or shaping the constant variability typical of such systems, be they mechanical, biological, or even social. The crucial feature of a control system is the closed feedback loop, whereby a given output is monitored and measured by a controlling device, with the information captured fed back into the controller in order to adjust, if need be, the inputs into the system. In contemporary industrialized societies, such mechanisms are not confined to workplaces, but are ubiquitous in everyday life, in such devices as cellphone cameras, automobile cruise controls, and air-conditioning thermostats. The earliest servomechanisms developed in the 1930s functioned by means of a constantly self-correcting feedback loop, in which data picked up by a sensor monitoring the change in a system were fed back into the control device, which adjusted automatically. Such closed-loop circuits were preceded, however, by the use of open-loop analogue computer systems in prewar petroleum refineries, electrical power plants, and chemical distilleries. These devices monitored and measured output and made often complex calculations using these data, but still required human operators to implement the indicated corrections; the operator himself made no "decisions" or

"calculations" with such a system, but merely implemented
a prescribed set of operations.

The implementation of automatic controls in industry from
the 1930s through the 1960s (and after) was therefore undertaken
in steps. The development and deployment of digital computers
in production, which used discrete rather than continuous signals,
and were much more precise than their analogue predecessors as
a result, has an ongoing history dating largely from the late 1950s.
The subsequent development of the automatic factory in the 1960s
required the use of digital computers and closed-loop feedback
devices, but even in these cases implementation was usually
restricted to single devices or units, such as computer numerical
control (CNC) machines. For much of the twentieth and well into
the twenty-first century, only the most advanced plants in certain
industries operated by means of a centralized automated control
of the entire factory complex. Even today, many factories in
traditional manufacturing industries, especially those operating
in low-wage regions, maintain high labor-to-capital ratios, and
use machinery with very primitive control devices, if they use
them at all.

Control devices were to replace human effort in and oversight
of the labor process. But this shorthand definition of automation,
which continues to be commonly used, misses much of the point
of the concept. The decisive factors in defining automation over
and against mechanization and rationalization are both the type
of human labor substituted for—the replacement of human
decision-making and oversight, rather than simple manual
operations—and, most importantly, the *integration* of formerly
discrete manufacturing operations so that the labor process is
transformed into a single, unbroken flow. Such "flow production,"
in which the product is assembled entirely without the intervention of human touch or activity, is predicated on what Marx
already described, in his account of the automatic factory, as a
maximal "continuity of production." Given this definition, it is

clear why highly automated production processes first developed in industries with liquid or gas products, such as in oil, electricity, and chemical plants, before later being applied to other branches of production such as metallurgy, mining, and automobile manufacturing. Where the conveyor-belt system often still required human labor to transport semi-finished products from workstation to workstation, to assemble the product itself, and to make decisions about starting and stopping machines, regulating temperature, pressure, flow rate, and so on, the idea—the dream—of the automated factory replaces all of these human roles and operations with ones performed by machines. Yet the idea of the fully automated factory, in which not only individual machines and work cells but an entire plant's operations—including purchasing, order processing, and the planning of production—would be regulated by feedback devices (primarily computers), remains largely that, an idea, even today. As recently as 1996, an observer could note that, in hindsight,

> applications in manufacturing have tended to be evolutionary. Looking back over the period since 1953, we see a continued application of the computer and control theory to manufacturing and manufacturing processes. However, with few exceptions, the automatic factory is still not widely realized.[16]

Friedrich Pollock's 1956 book on automation remains one of the most insightful contributions to the theory of automation that have surfaced in the postwar period. It is little known today. Pollock himself is best known as one of the founders of the famous Institute for Social Research in Frankfurt in 1923; later in that decade, he traveled to the Soviet Union and subsequently published a book on the experiments there with economic planning. With the rise of the Nazi regime in Germany, Pollock was compelled, along with his colleagues at the Institute, to emigrate to the United States; he returned to Frankfurt in 1950, and was appointed professor of economics at the University of Frankfurt a year later. A prolific writer, he was and remains best known for his 1941 essay on "state capitalism," in which he theorized the imminent replacement of nineteenth-century forms of liberal capitalism by command economies, in both democratic and "totalitarian" variants, in which the allocation of labor and capital would no longer be regulated by price signals but by political concerns and dictates, and carried out by means of a new, bureaucratic caste rather than private business owners.

Automation: A Study of Its Economic and Social Consequences, published in an Institute for Social Research book series on sociological questions, and arguably Pollock's most significant post-1945 work, is more modest in its objectives. It hints, on occasion, at themes from his earlier work, transposed to the postwar period. *Automation* briefly imagines, for example, a "new sort of society, based upon authoritarian or military principles" that would take shape with the prevalence of automated principles in production; it wonders whether in "a future 'automation society' the capitalists would either be absorbed by the leading group in society or they would lose their economic functions."[17] It concludes with a consideration of Norbert Wiener's then-recent claims regarding the political implications of automation techniques, only to reject them as exaggerated if not alarmist. The "widespread introduction of automation in industry," Pollock writes, will bring good with bad. What must be managed is the speed at which it is introduced, with a view not to the profitability of this or that industrial concern, but to the broader social consequences entailed: "The too rapid introduction of automation might bring with it a social catastrophe that only a totalitarian government would be strong enough to handle."[18]

The social catastrophe Pollock has in mind is *mass unemployment*. This was no idle concern for commentators of Pollock's generation. Writing from Frankfurt in the midst of Germany's postwar reconstruction and economic boom, the devastating effects of the Depression era must have weighed on him heavily. That had been an epoch, in many ways antithetical to the one he found himself in, marked by collapsing investment, a rash of business bankruptcies, deflation, and joblessness. In the U.S., this period had been marked by a sustained bout of worker militancy, in industry—the rise of the Congress of Industrial Organizations (CIO), the wave of sit-down strikes—and outside it. In Germany, these conditions gave rise to a prospective fascist exit from the crisis, one culminating in a conflagration laying waste to the European continent. "A study of recent history," Pollock writes, "can leave no doubt in anyone's mind that prolonged mass unemployment is the surest harbinger of totalitarian revolution." The fundamental responsibility of the political classes of the industrial democracies is therefore to head off any "totalitarian" antidote to the social wounds inflicted by a period of widespread worklessness. Rather than let workers, especially those who have no access to wage-paying work, take matters into their own hands, Pollock advises that "the government must at once take steps to remedy the situation as soon as unemployment figures rise above what the workers are likely to stand." Here the thrust of Pollock's postwar politics is made clear. The sole solution the working class itself can arrive at, once their tolerance for mass joblessness has been exceeded, is an authoritarian, indeed totalitarian, one. The state's mandate, therefore, is to act in the combined interests of the capitalist class and its partners in the large labor unions in order to thwart in advance any revolutionary remedy.

In his 1963 book *The American Revolution*, black factory worker and militant James Boggs describes what he understands to be the unique historical circumstances in which automation was introduced into factories in the automotive industry. "Automation," he writes, replaces men. This of course is nothing new. What *is* new is that now, unlike most earlier periods, *the displaced men have nowhere to go*. The farmers displaced by mechanization of the farms in the 20s could go to the cities and man the assembly lines. As for the work animals like the mule, they could just stop growing them. But automation displaces people, and you don't just stop growing people even when they have been made expendable by the system . . . the question of what to do with the surplus people who are the expendables of automation becomes more and more critical every day.[19]

The mechanization of agriculture, which dramatically raised agricultural productivity and rendered most farmworkers redundant, created a mobile mass of wage-laborers who had somewhere to go: the cities and the assembly lines of the North, the Midwest, and southern California. What would happen when a new wave of labor-saving efficiencies, this time driven not by the internal combustion engine but by CNC devices, swept over the massive production sites of the American automotive, steel, and petroleum industries?

Neither Pollock nor Boggs, neither union leadership nor the staffers assigned to Lyndon Johnson's National Commission on Technology, Automation, and Economic Progress quite foresaw what lay ahead. The capitalist economy itself provided the apparent solution to its own crisis of joblessness. The mass unemployment feared on all sides in the late 1950s and early 1960s was averted by a staggering and sustained expansion of the so-called service sector, which would soon absorb the vast majority of those workers displaced by automation in factories, while also taking in tens of millions of new entrants to the labor market: women.

By 1970, on the cusp of a new age defined by the refinements in computing capacity represented by the Intel 4004 processor, the achievements of the postwar wave of automation in industry meant that an ever-growing industrial output could be produced with ever-fewer workers. The percentage of u.s. workers in the manufacturing sector reached its postwar peak in June 1953, when a full third of u.s. workers were so classified. In 1970, after a decade in which American industry thrived and foreign competitors played catch-up, that number stood at less than a quarter of American workers. In 1990, it had fallen to 16 percent; by 2010, to 10 percent.[20] This shrinking share of manufacturing employment, however, was set against an explosion in the total number of workers active in the u.s. labor force. In 1953, they numbered only 62 million; in 1970, 15 million more. As of 1990, the total number of u.s. workers climbed to 120 million; by 2010, when manufacturing's employment share was flirting with single digits, the total was 140 million. It is still climbing. The share of workers now classified as working outside the manufacturing core of the u.s. economy has steadily increased since 1953: in relative terms, it has increased almost 50 percent. In absolute terms, the non-manufacturing sector tripled in size from 1953 to 2010, while the number of workers in manufacturing has actually declined from 20 to 15 million over the same span of time.

Significantly, women began to enter the workplace *en force* around 1970, by the tens of millions. As they did so, the nature of work itself began to change. In 1970, 32 million American women were counted as participating in the labor market; as of 1990, the number was 57 million (in 2009, 72 million).[21] Indeed, between 1970 and 2000, the labor force participation rate swelled dramatically, from 60 to 67 percent of the working age population; during this same period, the percentage of men actively employed or looking for work actually declined, from 79 to 74 percent (a number that has continued to decline dramatically since).[22] As women began pouring into labor markets in the u.s., they often found work in clerical and business services, in healthcare, education, and retail. One effect of this wholesale entry of women into workplaces was to accelerate the commodification of personal services previously carried out in the form of unwaged, domestic labor.

Between 1970 and 1990, the rhetoric of job-killing automation so prevalent from the mid-1950s well into the 1960s tapered off dramatically. Yet as business investment in new "information" technologies ramped up in the early 1990s, with refined bar code and radio-frequency identification (RFID) tracking technologies making possible important innovations in supply chain and inventory management, the volume of chatter about "automation" began to rise once again. Typical was a 1994 article from the *Wall Street Journal*, which breathlessly recycled an old tune from the early 1960s: "technological advances are now so rapid that companies can shed far more workers than they need to hire to implement the technology or support expanding sales."[23] Jeremy Rifkin felt comfortable calling his 1995 book *The End of Work*, even as he remained circumspect enough to push back the arrival of a "nearly automated" service sector until the mid-twenty-first century:

> This much we know for sure: We are entering into a new period in history where machines will increasingly replace human labor in the production of goods and services. Although timetables are difficult to predict, we are set on a firm course to an automated future and will likely approach a near-workerless era, at least in manufacturing, by the early decades of the coming century. The service sector, while slower to automate, will probably approach a nearly automated state by the mid-decades of the next century.[24]

Since the publication of Rifkin's prediction, millions more workers have entered the service sector in high-income countries as manufacturing employment has contracted still further.

Over the past two decades, nineteen of twenty new jobs in the U.S. have been in what Matthew Klein calls

> sectors known to have low productivity . . . and sectors where low productivity is merely suspected . . . Since 2000, *94 per cent* of the net jobs created were in education, healthcare, social assistance, bars, restaurants, and retail, even though those sectors only employed 36 per cent of America's work-force at the start of the millennium."[25]

It is jobs like these, Rifkin speculated, that would have to be replaced by machines if the labor productivity figures that puzzle economists and policy-makers are to wake from their current and long-standing slumber. A new wave of automation would have to overtake restaurants, retail, and distribution hubs; it would have to decimate employment in accounting, legal services, and finance; labor-intensive occupations that require significant face-to-face interaction between consumers and employees, like nursing and teaching, would all have to be subject to complete reformatting along properly industrial lines, losing their handicraft aspect, to ensure rising labor productivity on a par with the achievements witnessed in the manufacturing sector two generations ago.

This is the prospect envisaged by studies like those published by the Oxford Martin School, warning of the replacement of half of U.S. workers by machines. Have we finally reached the moment in the historical development of capitalism in which James Boggs's words—"What is new is that now, unlike most earlier periods, the displaced men have nowhere to go"—ring true?

two

The Robot and the Zombie

After the grand wave of inventions which between 1910 and 1940 brought in the automobile, the aeroplane, the refrigerator, the television, and so on, significant invention practically petered out. Improvement, refinement, packaging—anything to enhance the prestige of the object, but nothing by way of structural innovation.

—JEAN BAUDRILLARD, *The System of Objects*[1]

Since the early 1970s, trends in labor productivity across the advanced economies of the world, and exemplarily those of the U.S., the UK, and Japan, has experienced a steady and inexorable decline, with only a parenthetical uptick in the mid-1990s. The onset of the 2008 crisis only exacerbated the trend. Since 2010, productivity gains in manufacturing in particular have been disconcertingly weak. Yet, for reasons that will be examined below, it was at the nadir of the crisis—at a moment in which labor productivity gains were lower than they'd been since the beginnings of the Industrial Age—that books and articles proclaiming ours a "time of brilliant technologies" began to appear everywhere. *The Second Machine Age*, written by two professors at MIT's Sloan School of Management, was not an outlier among them in claiming that the "full force" of contemporary technologies had been "achieved." Defining these technologies in the broadest of strokes as "digital" ones, and more specifically as "networked digital devices running an astonishing array of software," Brynjolfsson and McAfee built their case primarily on the modest business resurgence of the late 1990s; they stretched this episode beyond the fierce collapse of the dotcom bubble, alleging that the "first five years of the twenty-first century saw a renewed wave of innovation and investment." Yet confronted with what they called "the recent slowdown" that, at the time of the book's publication, was at its most severe point, the authors tried out an array of responses, attributing the pause not only to the ongoing recession but more broadly to two potentially incompatible causes: immeasurability and "lags" in the diffusion of these technologies. On the one hand, the argument goes, the gains aren't being captured by the conventional metrics used by statisticians to gauge changes in categories like GDP and productivity. Measuring productivity in services like healthcare and education is particularly difficult, where "improvements" in care or instruction are hard to pin down with statistics. On the other hand, as fully formed as these technologies are, they have not yet been adapted by a sufficient number of users to realize their full impact on the economy and everyday life. The "fundamentals are in place," the authors enthused, "for [a] bounty that vastly exceeds anything we've ever seen before."[2]

Yet, still today in 2020, few verdicts on the course of the past few decades have had as much resonance as that pronounced by the economist Robert Solow more than thirty years ago, at the conclusion of a July 1987 book review. There, in a seemingly off-handed remark, Solow noted that "what everyone feels to have been a technological revolution"—he is alluding to advances in computing technology since the late 1960s— has "been accompanied everywhere by a slowing-down of productivity growth, not by a step up. You can see the computer age everywhere but in the productivity statistics."[3] Solow spoke with some authority: that same year, he was awarded the Nobel Prize for his contributions to the field of economics.

In 1982, largely in response to the recent availability of personal computers, *Time* had designated the computer "Machine of the Year." Large, inefficient analogue computers had been around for half a century, and employed in industry since the 1930s; digital computers came online and in broad use much later, in the 1960s. The breakthrough in the development of computing power arrived with the production, in 1970, of the Intel 4004 single-chip silicon microprocessor; advances in semiconductor design proceeded with great rapidity thereafter. As early as 1965, Intel cofounder Gordon Moore postulated what would be loosely deemed a "law" governing technological change in the field of semiconductors and computer hardware: every two years, twice the number of transistors can be fitted onto a single chip, while the costs of production are halved.[4] Engineers have indeed succeeded in packing more and more circuits onto an individual chip; the exponential growth of computing capacity, combined with steep drops in microprocessor prices, has been dizzying, the predicted pattern largely unbroken over decades. This leap forward in microprocessor design did not occur in a void. It was accompanied by significant discoveries in biotechnology and composite materials. Refinements in fiber optics occurred in concert with those in semiconductors. In 1983, Corning managed to produce these thin glass threads more cheaply than copper wire, which they have largely replaced in many uses. The progress made on these two fronts—microprocessors and optical fiber—shaped the world Solow saw around him. The mating of these innovations constitutes no small part of what is novel even about our technological horizon in 2020. These were palpable achievements. Their intertwining makes up much of the current mediascape: streaming video, billions-strong social networks, financial transactions zapped across the world in fractions of a second.

Solow's troubled observation that the pace of technological change was not matched by efficiencies in labor productivity has come to be known as the "productivity paradox." The dilemma has become only more pronounced and perplexing since 2000, as productivity gains have tapered off still more. In the UK the puzzle of the productivity gap is worried over time and again in the public press, especially in the crisis environment, and alongside claimed breakthroughs in artificial intelligence and machine learning. Even Brynjolfsson and McAfee have had to hedge their bets. They remind us, in the small print, that it took "nearly a century for the benefits of electrification" to come to full flower.[5]

In the years just after Solow's pronouncement, however, a sophisticated version of this response to those "perplexed by the conjuncture of rapid technological innovation with disappointingly slow gains in measured productivity" was mounted, by an economist at Stanford named Paul A. David.[6] In a 1990 article in the *American Economic Review*, David framed the phantom productivity burst expected from the widespread use of "the computer chip"—the term "automation" is not used once—by means of a potent historical analogy with the electric dynamo, invented a century before.

The analogy with the computer is clear enough. The dynamo and the computer both operate as what David calls "nodal elements" in distributed networks; their transformative effects are fully felt once a threshold in the number of users is reached. David notes that it was only in the late teens that the diffusion level of centralized power production reached 50 percent. Computer-driven information and communication technology is, in turn, a "general-purpose engine" along the lines of Watt's steam engine (1780s) and the dynamo (1880s): a once-in-a-century revolutionary technology that will affect not this or that industry, or one economic sector among others, but the economy as a whole and society more generally. The conversion to the power grid required not simply the complete redesign of factories and production facilities; it entailed the elaboration of entirely new infrastructural networks, and would remake urban conglomerations from top to bottom. The electrification of the factory not only facilitated the "rationalization" of industrial labor processes in the 1920s, it made possible the first adumbrations of continuous flow production techniques in the 1930s, as well as the application of primitive breakthroughs in feedback-based "control" systems in production: "advances in automatic process control engineering were dependent upon use of electrical instrumentation and electro-mechanical relays."[7] The introduction of electricity into individual households—in 1920, it was present in only one-third of u.s. households; by 1930, excluding farms, the number was over 80 percent[8]—would make possible the use of domestic appliances on a mass scale in the postwar period, raising the productivity of unwaged, domestic labor. If ever there was a revolutionary "general purpose engine," it was the dynamo and the electrical grid. It is the top-to-bottom impact of this technology that accounts for the lag—the decades-long gap—between its invention and its full implementation.

The obstacles standing in the way of this revolution were stubborn indeed. This particular general-purpose technology was initially developed, after all, in the midst of the crippling, sustained economic crisis of 1873–96. Under such conditions, defined by depressed profit rates and skittish investors, private firms were not able or willing to undertake significant and costly revisions of their still functional production lines. Even with the conclusion of the crisis in the mid-1890s, two decades after its onset, the manufacturing sector in both the u.s. and the uk remained listless, dormant. Often perceived as a period of plenty—a horizonless British Empire, a *belle époque*—the decades after the crisis were defined all the same by a "pronounced slowdown in industrial and aggregate productivity growth experienced during the 1890–1913 era by the two leading industrial countries, Britain and the United States."[9] The deferred adoption of new technologies, which promised labor-saving efficiencies, was due in large part to the time required to build out the infrastructure necessary to support it. Fixed capital represents a sunk cost it takes years to earn back, as a given combination of plant and equipment transfers its value piecemeal to the goods it produces, depreciating over a period not of years but decades. Though by the turn of the century economies were able to get out from under the dark cloud of the first downturn to be called "the great depression," and business owners found cheap lines of credit extended to them once again, these changing conditions did not affect the primitive arithmetic of industrialists, who confronted the "unprofitability of replacing still serviceable manufacturing plants embodying production technologies adapted to the old regime of mechanical power derived from water and steam."[10] It would take the extraordinary episode of a global war, combined with the eventual obsolescence of these older facilities, to launch what David, following the British-Venezuelan Schumpeterian economist Carlota Perez, calls a new "technological regime."

Seductive as David's historical analogy is, the claim it makes stands or falls on the historical record. The three decades since it was written have pronounced their verdict. Why haven't the cluster of innovations (or the general-purpose engine) sometimes referred to as information and communication technologies (ICT), despite indubitable advances in technical and material capacity, yielded a 1920s-like boom in economic output and efficiency? David's argument presumes that what we now call automation (rather than "the computer chip") is analogous to dynamo-driven centralized electricity, and that the period beginning in the early 1970s and extending through the 1980s resembles the social and economic conditions prevailing during the two decades flanking the turn of the twentieth century. It is true that in each case a key process innovation was discovered in an age of sustained stagnation; the Intel 4004 microprocessor, like the dynamo, was produced at the onset of an enduring crisis. But labor productivity for the entire period spanning the subsequent two decades leading up to the date of David's publication barely budged.

The explosion in productivity unleashed by the wide use of the electrical grid—assisted, in turn, by the internal combustion engine—was well underway by the 1920s, forty years after the first dynamo appeared. Indeed, despite David's contention that both the U.S. and the UK experienced a "pronounced slowdown in industrial and aggregate productivity growth . . . during the 1890–1913 era," most commentators suggest this is *not* the case: that is, that one of the peculiarities of the long depression of the late nineteenth century was its economic dynamism, with little falloff in industrial output and productivity from the boom of the previous business cycle.[11] No similar pattern can be found for the advanced economies of North America and Europe, over the past half-century. Since the turn of the century, these economies have been marked not by a long-awaited surge in labor productivity, but by stagnation and decline across the board, in both the rate of labor productivity gains and in investment in ICT by private businesses, despite an equities boom driven by so-called technology companies. Now, a full fifty years after the invention of the Intel 4004 chip, we can legitimately ask: was the brief productivity surge of the late 1990s, occurring before the global ramification of the Internet and the rise of "smart" phones, factories, and cities, all we'll get?

David's postulation of a diffusion lag to explain Solow's productivity paradox relies implicitly on a "long wave" analysis of patterns of economic development, positing a rhythm of capitalist expansion and contraction longer than the roughly decade-long rhythm of the classical business cycle. This style of analysis, favored also by some Marxist economists, has found a more explicit echo in Paul Mason's *Postcapitalism: A Guide to Our Future* (2015). Mason, like David, locates the deep, driving force of these epochal patterns of accumulation, marked by roughly 25-year periods of alternating flourishing and decline, in changes of technological "regime." Technological regimes are defined not simply by a single revolutionary or general purpose technology, but by clusters of innovation that fuse together to force forward a top-to-bottom social transformation: in "business models, skill-sets, markets, currencies, technologies."[12] Mason follows the lead of Ernest Mandel in emphasizing the explanatory power of so-called Kondratieff waves, named after a Russian economist who claimed to identify a set of long-term cyclical patterns of economic development in the early 1920s, on the basis of an analysis of a century's worth of published data on commodity prices, wages, and interest rates. The value of these discoveries was hotly debated throughout the 1920s and left their mark on both Kondratieff's critic Leon Trotsky and on Joseph Schumpeter's 1939 book on business cycles.

These debates centered both on the reality of the proposed recurring patterns of upswing and decline, and on the causal underpinnings of these changes. Since Kondratieff remained agnostic on the latter question in particular, others stepped in to offer their accounts. Trotsky appealed to contingent, extra-economic shocks like wars, revolutions, and colonial conquests; Schumpeter also sought an Archimedean point outside the endogenous motions of capital accumulation, pointing instead to changes in technological constellations. A former Trotskyist and newscaster, currently a ubiquitous public intellectual close to former British Labour Party leader Jeremy Corbyn, Mason follows the Schumpeterian line. By his calculations, the long downturn dating from 1973 should have exhausted itself after 35 years, around 2008, succeeded by a sustained upswing. Instead, we got a decade described by the Bank of England as "the worst . . . since the late 18th century" in terms of aggregate productivity growth.[13] Mason's central idea is that the cyclical upswing we should have gotten has been thwarted by the power of financial capital.

The claims made by Mason in *Postcapitalism* compete with the hyperbole of the business-school professors who wrote *The Second Machine Age*. Where Brynjolfsson and McAfee speak of an age of "brilliant technologies" promising a "bounty that vastly exceeds anything we've ever seen before," Mason surveys the wreckage of the last quarter-century and intones that, "if we consider not just info-tech but food processing, birth control or global health, the past twenty-five years have probably seen the greatest upsurge in human capability ever." Despite the crushing impact of the ongoing economic meltdown, particularly in austerity-blighted Britain, the crisis years themselves witnessed, he observes, a "rapid rollout out of new technologies" without precedent in a deep depression, "in a way that just didn't happen in the 1930s": this, despite the fact that it was precisely in that decade that the control technologies responsible for the postwar automation of core industries were developed.[14] Our age of brilliant technologies should, therefore, have launched a new epoch defined not by ongoing turmoil and disarray but by "*an exponential takeoff in productivity* and the extensive automation of physical processes," had it been able to throw off the coils of a "system of monopolies, banks and governments struggling to maintain control over power and information."[15]

Here Mason has turned the world on its head. If ours is an age defined by monopolies, cheap credit, rent-seeking, and asset bubbles, it is not due to the concerted efforts of elites keen to forestall or smother in the cradle a new, sustained period of productivity gains and extensive automation of labor processes. To the contrary, it is with these very elites—the system of monopolies, banks, and governments—that the promise of such a "takeoff" originates, a promise which Mason here echoes, elaborates, and amplifies. Despite claims to the contrary, the weather of stagnation and drift that has settled over the advanced capitalist economies since the 1970s, and especially since the turn of the century, is attributable in no small part to sustained technological inertia.

Technological Stagnation

The surge of innovations that, combined, brought about the so-called second industrial revolution had a profound effect on the patterns of daily life and on productive capacity in the workplace. We have already looked at the transformations induced by the cheap energy made possible by the electric dynamo and its gridded delivery networks. Developments in the distribution of energy were matched by advances in its production. The discovery of the techniques necessary for the extraction and refinement of crude oil in the second half of the nineteenth century would have enormous, and largely unforeseen, consequences for the following century. Few features of the twentieth century's dynamism would be untouched by these innovations. In addition to being a primary source of energy unleashing the productive capacities of industrialized nations, the ready availability of new fuels (gasoline, diesel) accelerated improvements in the internal combustion engine; the tracing out of vast road networks would inevitably supplement and complete this breakthrough. The material used to pave these surfaces is itself a petroleum by-product, asphalt; by the middle of the twentieth century, a dizzying array of petroleum-derived materials, from plastics to polyester, with their distinct textures and colors, would compose the decor of modernity. Advances in oil refinement can be seen as merely one front in a broader set of discoveries in the natural sciences, in particular in the manipulation of chemical structure, which led to the development of synthetic materials and dyes, and to revolutionary leaps forward in the concoction of medicines, and the eventual rise of the pharmaceutical industry.

The last decade and a half of the nineteenth century witnessed more than one epoch-defining innovation in the field of telecommunications (radio, telephone) and imaging techniques (popular photography, motion pictures). The signal technological breakthrough of the past two decades—the circulation of images across networked computer terminals—represents little more than the splicing together of these two long-extant technologies. Where the innovations of the second industrial revolution reshaped the coming century from top to bottom, transforming both the workplace and day-to-day life, the emblematic technologies of the current epoch, like the smartphone, represent little more than a "better" version—more compact and convenient, with more computing power—of already available devices.[16] The primary innovation offered by the Apple iPhone is the layering into a single device of an array of by-now near-ancient technologies: a twenty-first-century Swiss Army knife, combining the telephone, personal computer, camera and video recorder in a single, pocket-sized, consumer good. As such examples suggest, the technologies characteristic of the past two decades—since the dotcom crash of 2000—have been concentrated in entertainment and leisure: toys, not tools. The smartphone, social media, CGI, and video games, icons of the contemporary moment, have little purchase or effect on workplaces; they can be safely assimilated, instead, to what older theories called "the spectacle," a cluster of diversionary gadgets. Rather than an economy-wide adoption of a cluster of recent innovations (fiber optics, silicon microprocessors, solar energy) resulting in harvested productivity gains and a revolution-ized everyday life, the meager results of the third industrial revolution—or "the second machine age"—have been less exhilarating: a tsunami of infantilizing gadgets that double as tracking collars for adults and children alike. These technical devices function, for the most part, "chiefly for public amusement or mystification," to cite Andrew Ure once again. "However admirable as exercises of mechanical science," they "do nothing towards the supply of the physical necessities of society."

Social media platforms and search engines, their ubiquity notwithstanding, represent in economic terms little other than extremely refined advertising delivery systems that reach billions of users. Google's parent company Alphabet speaks in exalted tones of technological moonshots, but 90 percent of its revenue and almost all of its profits still come from product placement, most of it via search engines. Facebook, which claims to host 2.5 billion users, derives a full 97 percent of its revenue from ad placement on its array of social media platforms (Facebook, Instagram, WhatsApp, etc.); like Google, it has one of the highest market capitalizations in the world, dwarfing the traditional companies offering goods and services—Starbucks, Visa, and Nike—to which it sells ads. (Most of this revenue is derived from mobile smartphone users.) Ridesharing platforms like Uber and Lyft rely on a technology that has existed for a century, the private automobile; they are little more than unregulated, cheap taxi services. No productivity gains are delivered by its digitally mediated arrangements. Its users travel the same roads, at the same speeds, carrying the same number of passengers as do all other automobiles. Uber and Lyft own no vehicles, and employ no drivers; like AirBnB, they provide an advertising medium for individuals providing services, for which they charge exorbitant fees. The "technology" here is primarily the breaking of the traditional work contract, the employee transformed into a self-employed (yet intensely monitored) freelancer; the platform connects users and providers in the marketplace, and takes a cut of every transaction, charging a toll from both parties for the privilege of using it. These companies, whose revenues take the form of rents derived from ownership and control of their platforms, and whose users provide, along with payment, free data in exchange for the services the companies provide, can be considered crisis-period phenomena.[17] Coming into their own since 2012 and after, such platforms are at best novel business models, not innovative technologies; their inherently monopolistic format and their unproductive siphoning of revenue via product placement or transaction fees are, arguably, a hindrance to technological disruption, a rearguard *barrage* retarding rather than embodying innovation.[18]

When we learn that the most successful new product in years offered by Apple, whose market cap recently exceeded the trillion-dollar threshold, was a pair of wireless earphones, we are right to sense a mismatch between the ambitious rhetoric of tech companies and the trinkets with which they flood the market. It is hard to imagine that "information technology," billed in

Martin Ford's *The Rise of the Robots* as a "truly general-purpose technology" on a par with steam or the electrical dynamo, is anything of the sort; despite the unleashed power of ramped-up computing capacity, with vast networks linking phones and laptops into global webs transmitting billions of texts and images, videos, and voices second-by-second, the age of the computer has turned out to be a dud. Even with its later iterations, rebranded as automation, AI, machine learning, and so on, no turnaround for a crisis-mired global economy has been in the offing. Instead, surrounded by screens, keypads, sensors, and CCTV cameras, the networked individuals of the richest regions of the planet produce barely more goods and services than their equals did at the turn of the century; the capitalist economy, without peer or rival since the vanquishing of the Second World and the entry of Chinese millions into global labor markets, has sputtered and lurched from crisis to crisis—financial panics, currency scares, mortgage rate defaults, indeed, IT bubbles—for fifty years. A pattern dating, coincidentally, from the very moment the silicon microprocessor and its promises were delivered unto the world.

Declining Investment

The widely held premise that the world's advanced economies are poised at a tipping point, on the threshold of a new epoch of dynamism, growth, and rising prosperity, presupposes that these same economies have demonstrated rising rates of investment in R&D and fixed capital in recent decades. If there is a "lag" in the broad distribution and implementation of these socially trans- formative technologies, private companies competing against one another must scramble to develop and incorporate any competitive advantage that offers itself; the application of "automation" across the vast service sector should, it seems, be reformatting labor processes, giving rise to a surge in labor productivity for adopters of these innovations, as well as compelling transformations in corporate and capital structures. The claims of some commentators notwithstanding, there is little evidence of any such wave of significant investment in ICT since the early 1990s (which produced a short-term boost in labor productivity that was largely over by 2000). In his rich and provocative *The Rise and Fall of American Growth*, economist Robert Gordon demonstrates instead that, since the turn of the century, the U.S. economy has seen a rapid *falloff* in net investment by private firms. The data are disturbing, or perplexing, for those who wish to promote the present epoch as a period of rapid and profound change, a technological turning point. Beginning in 1950, *Rise and Fall* tracks the ratio of "net investment" to capital stock—the money companies have spent on capital items, whether plant and property or, more pointedly, information and communication technologies—up to the present, with surprising findings: The rate of net investment by U.S. companies peaked around 1970, from which point it has declined; since 2002, however, such investment has fallen dramatically. Though the rate of net investment over the period 1950 to 2007 averages out to 3.2 percent, it has broken this threshold only once since the late 1980s, during the dotcom "boom"; in the early 1990s, just before that boom, it dipped to 2 percent. In 2013, in the full flower of the post-2008 "recovery," and as tech companies cemented their dominance of equity markets and leisure time in the richest countries, it had plummeted to just 1 percent, "less than a third of the 3.2 percent 1950–2007 average."[19]

A recent study by J. W. Mason finds similar patterns and draws similar conclusions. Focusing especially on the crisis-ravaged landscape of the past decade, Mason rightly wonders whether any "recovery" has taken place during this period, despite proclamations that date its starting point as early as 2009. He notes that official assessments identifying the end of the recession are founded on a single variable: the cessation, sustained over two quarters, of declines in GDP. In short, recessions stop when the bleeding does. This does not mean that pre-crisis trendlines resume, only that we are at the bottom of the abyss. To rejoin those earlier trendlines, weak as they already were, requires years, assuming everything goes well. In this case all did not go well. Mason, like Gordon, emphasizes the historically slow productivity growth of this period and, examining possible causes for this slowdown, highlights one salient feature of the "recovery": "exceptionally weak investment spending." Indeed, his study underlines that there is simply "no precedent for the weakness of investment in the current cycle"; it is not only slow relative to an already "anemic" pace of GDP growth, but is "extremely low by historical standards."[20]

It gets worse. Mason notes that, dispiriting as they are, these data actually hide how low investment in technological "innovation" has been over this decade. Because recently changed accounting conventions allow companies to count "intellectual property [IP] production" as investment spending, existing data for private investment now incorporate expenditures targeting the protection of revenue flows secured through legal title to technologies and processes, rather than the invention or refinement of newer, more efficient labor processes or organizational schemas. In fact, "during the most recent cycle, business spending on IP production has been considerably stronger than other forms of investment," and the inclusion of this form of spending alongside improvements in production blurs the distinction between two very different types of "investment": the dynamism typical of highly competitive industries and sectors requiring constant innovation, and the stagnation typical of non-competitive ones, where market share is secured through protection of proprietary technologies (and the streams of data and revenue they generate). If we remove this "regressive" type of spending from aggregate investment numbers, so as to isolate expenditures on "plant and equipment plus R&D," "the current expansion looks even weaker at only 7 percent above the 2007 peak."[21]

What is more, the large technology companies, from which we might expect the most liberal outlays for research and product development, often count as "investment" the snapping up of smaller companies that might pose competitive threats for market share down the road; rather than incorporate and develop the technologies and innovations these upstarts have begun, all-powerful Silicon Valley megafirms like Apple and Alphabet buy them out in order to relegate them to their margins, preferring they die on the vine. The former chief economist for the IMF, Harvard's Kenneth Rogoff, notes that

> Big Tech firms might argue that all the capital they pour into new products and services is pushing innovation. One suspects, however, that in many circumstances the intent is to nip potential competition in the bud. It is notable that Big Tech still derives most of its revenues from its companies' core products—for example, the Apple iPhone, Microsoft Office, and the Google search engine. Thus, in practice, potentially disruptive new technologies are as likely to be buried as nourished.[22]

Who or what, exactly, is Big Tech? Though the vast, monopoly-type corporations now seem like wallpaper to citizens of the U.S., Europe, and beyond, so ubiquitous are their names and products in news feeds if not always in people's daily lives, and so naturalized is their outsized social presence, their preeminence dates from less than a decade ago: Big Tech is an outgrowth of a still unrelenting crisis. In the first quarter of 2007, the ten publicly traded companies with the largest market capitalization included multinational corporations from a range of economic sectors, featuring manufacturing, oil and natural gas, telecommunications, and banking. These companies were headquartered in five different countries (the U.S., Japan, China, Russia, the Netherlands), and included some of the most recognizable company names of the last forty years: Exxon, Shell, GE, Toyota, and AT&T. In 2007, only one of what are now called the "Big Tech" firms made the list (Microsoft); today, the top seven slots are occupied by such firms, the first five nominally U.S. companies, the other two, Chinese. Apple entered the list in the last quarter of 2009, as the "recovery" began, its market cap less than $200 billion. Today, holding the top spot, it is worth five times that.[23] The iPhone was first marketed in late 2007, as the crisis set in. By 2014 Apple was worth half a trillion dollars on paper; a year later, three-quarters of a trillion. Throughout this period, its core products remained a set of "smart" devices (iPhone, iPad, iPod), an expansive network of retail stores, and a lucrative service-provisioning division. Its recent triumphs in equities markets, like those of its peer "Big Tech" companies Facebook and Google, have come despite very little innovation in either product development or organizational efficiencies. Throughout the crisis period, unlike firms across the economy as a whole, Apple has piled up profits; by February 2018 the company held cash reserves of $300 billion.[24] Yet instead of investing these profits in product innovation or expanding existing capacity, Apple has chosen to spend an astonishing $210 billion since 2012 on stock buybacks, a full $100 billion of it in 2018, as a windfall from the $1.5 trillion dollar tax cuts passed by Congress flooded into their coffers. Many other cash-rich corporations followed suit. According to the Roosevelt Institute, corporations spent $3 out of every $5 of their net profit on stock repurchases between 2015 and 2017; some $1.1 trillion in corporate profits (with Apple leading the way) was spent on buybacks by the end of 2018.[25]

These purchases drive up equity price shares in the open market, rewarding existing shareholders by redistributing profits in the form of inflated asset prices as shares are taken out of circulation. The net effect of such buybacks is, many observers have suggested, to "starve" investment; rather than pour record profits into purchases of fixed capital, cash is disgorged in the form of payouts to shareholders. An August 2018 editorial in the *New York Times*, published as announced corporate stock buybacks were set to shatter the previous record (from 2007), emphasized that this practice "leaves [these businesses] that much less to invest in new production, or wages. In fact, *spending on business equipment* [has] *slowed*."[26] The *Washington Post* made the same point in an analysis from June 8, 2018:

> Today's economic boom is driven not by any great burst of innovation or growth in productivity . . . Corporate executives and directors are apparently bereft of ideas and the confidence to make long-term investments. Rather than using record profits, and record amounts of borrowed money, to invest in new plants and equipment, develop new products, improve service, lower prices or raise the wages and skills of their employees, they are "returning" that money to shareholders. Corporate America, in effect, has transformed itself into one giant leveraged buyout. Consider Apple, the world's most valuable enterprise. As a result of a $100 billion share buyback announced last month, Apple will have returned $210 billion to shareholders since 2012. How much is $210 billion? As Robin Wigglesworth of the *Financial Times* reminded his Twitter followers, that's enough to buy up the bottom 480 companies of the S&P 500.[27]

In the first half of 2018, as stock market indexes (especially the tech-heavy NASDAQ) blew through historical highs, a total of six companies, all usually lumped in the category of the "tech"—or, more broadly, the "Internet"—sector, generated a full 99 percent of the S&P 500 index's gains for the year.[28] The simple subtraction of the FAANG companies (Facebook, Amazon, Apple, Netflix, and Alphabet's Google), along with Microsoft, from the index would leave a group of 494 large-cap companies that have generated net zero growth in equity prices over the first six months of 2018.[29]

One of the distinguishing features of contemporary technology and "Internet" companies is that their success depends on the exploitation of network effects. Their primary assets are their users, the myriad connections that form between them, and the capture of the information their exchanges generate. The most powerful networks are those that incorporate the most users, and those that render competing networks irrelevant by starving them of those same users. Convincing users to sign on to a given network or platform often means making access to the territory staked out by a given networked service—rideshares, search engines, social media—free, in exchange for exclusive access to the data generated by users. The business model put in place by these companies relies therefore on the practice of so-called "cross-subsidization," in which a company provides a specific good or service for free (or at below market price or cost of production) in order to lock in users; the provisioning of this free service will, the company hopes, be paid out of profits generated from the externalities networks entail. Losing hundreds of millions of dollars upfront in the process of establishing dominance over a given market is normal in such scenarios. The long play is rarely if ever to invest in cheaper, better services in a marketplace defined by vigorous competition between rival firms, each looking for, and investing resources in producing, efficiencies and innovation. The goal is to create, eventually, a monopoly-like environment, either by underbidding competitors and absorbing enormous losses for years, or by snapping up potential competitors before they can establish themselves as genuine threats. Companies able to clear the field, so as to be the "last man standing," are entitled to rent-like revenues shaped not by the energies of competitive markets but by the prerogatives due the victors. The few "superstar" firms that are driving the current equities bubble attract investors with the promise of de facto, or eventual, super-profits of the sort banked by companies powerful enough to control entire economic sectors.[30]

And what of all the other firms grinding their way through the crisis, firms not accorded the superstar status bestowed on enormous, toll-collecting platforms? The crisis environment of the past decade has, paradoxically, given a new lease on life to loser companies that should have been swept out with the crisis tide, but have held on under historically exceptional circumstances. A recent study published by the OECD observes the "increasing survival" over the past decade of what it calls "zombie firms," non-competitive companies that under normal market conditions would be killed off by more innovative and efficient rivals. They are called zombies because they are in effect dead, kept "alive" only by the availability of historically low borrowing rates. Zombie firms are usually older companies that have trouble generating enough revenue to service their debt: they are typically defined as firms whose operating profits remain, year-over-year, less than their annual debt service payments. Because the price of credit during the crisis period has been unprecedentedly low, these companies have been able to muddle through much longer than they should, often treading water by repeatedly refinancing existing debt. Such companies became commonplace in Japan's lost decade of the 1990s, but have made a particularly strong comeback on a global scale since the onset of the crisis, as central banks everywhere flooded the capital markets with cheap money in a desperate attempt to jumpstart private spending. The ability of such low-productivity companies to hang on through a diet of cheap credit has a number of dele-terious effects, since the extension of credit to them is by definition a suboptimal allocation of resources. In particular, the survival of such firms often means the crowding out of opportunities for other, potentially more dynamic firms, including younger firms that lose out on access to the capital and market share afforded their undead, aging peers: "resources sunk in zombie firms have risen since the mid-2000s and the increasing survival of these low productivity firms at the margins of exit congests markets and constrains the growth of more productive firms."[31]

The two characteristic business models of the post-2008 crisis period are thus the platform and the zombie. The composition of the global economy consists of a few eminent companies, swarmed by legions of companies condemned to a ghostly existence on the edges: "a handful of cash-rich mega caps are masking significant problems elsewhere" in the corporate sector.[32] An enormous chasm has opened between the top 5 percent of u.s. corporations, which are thriving in the crisis environment, and the rest. Indeed, a mere thirty American companies are today responsible for a full half of the total profits among publicly traded companies. While the leading companies, many of them "tech" companies that are cash-rich but with little expectation of significant returns on productive investment, use their revenues to purchase their own shares, "invest" in intellectual property, or squash future competitors through mergers and acquisitions, much of the rest of the corporate sector ekes out an existence, making ends meet through cheap financing. This has led to an extraordinary surge in corporate borrowing rates during the crisis decade, now at unprecedented levels. Recessions, particularly deep ones, have historically been marked by corporate deleveraging; yet, by 2016, the total outstanding debt burdens for the large cap firms of the s&p 500 had reached dizzying, historic levels. Worse still, the type of debt being issued to corporations has increasingly taken the form of so-called "covenant-lite" financing, the corporate equivalent of subprime mortgage loans: 85 percent of outstanding corporate debt is the equivalent of junk financing, compared to a mere 30 percent in 2007 (the numbers are just as high in Europe as in the u.s.). Outside of a few superstar firms, then, lurk a multitude of companies a downturn away from defaulting on these mountains of debt; in not only the u.s., but Europe, India, Korea, and China. The coming depression will, more likely than not, have its origins in this enormous pile of junk financing, so much dry tinder awaiting its spark.

three

Army of Shadows

From 2007, 10-year average productivity growth was negative for the first time in almost a century. Overall, it was the worst decade since the late 18th century.

—Bank of England, April 2018[1]

When on June 1, 2018 the u.s. Department of Labor released its monthly report on the American labor market, the response was especially enthusiastic. Not since the turn of the century, in the midst of the most significant economic uptick in decades—and an historically unprecedented stock market bubble—had unemployment figures registered so low. The dwindling number of those who claimed to be still searching for work was particularly significant for a u.s. economy that had seen joblessness skyrocket, predictably, in the wake of the 2008 economic crisis. Though that crisis, as noted in the previous chapter, was said to have ended in June 2009, the recovery remained modest at best for years. Especially slow to respond to the apparent good news was the labor market. The official rate of unemployment peaked at 10 percent in late 2009 and hovered in the high single digits for a half-decade more; it crossed the threshold of 5 percent only at the beginning of the 2016 presidential election year. The decline in joblessness has proceeded apace, the rate steadily nosing downward. The ascent of Donald Trump to the American presidency seems, if only by coincidence, to have hastened this dwindling of what Marx called the "reserve army" of the unemployed. In his first year and a half in office, from January 2017 to May 2018, a full 1 percent downtick in unemployment was reported by the Bureau of Labor Statistics (BLS). In a typical if particularly ecstatic response to this news, the *New York Times* was left speechless by the jaw-dropping numbers: "We Ran Out of Words to Describe How Good the Jobs Numbers Are" was the title the paper of record placed over one assessment of these figures, and the underlying and resurgent dynamism of the U.S. economy they suggest.[2]

One word the *Times* could not, in a show of prudence, bring itself to pronounce in describing an otherwise "bustling" economy was "perfect," though by thrusting that word forward it is clear the temptation was real. "It isn't perfect," the paper's senior economics correspondent wrote, noting with a hint of due caution that the numbers might not tell the whole story. On the one hand, "wage growth remains unexceptional"; on the other hand, the share of "prime-age adults working remains below its historical levels."

As often happens on the heels of such bursts of euphoria, a letdown soon set in. The wait was not long. Just two weeks after the job numbers were posted, the very same U.S. Department of Labor confirmed that over the year-long period beginning in May 2017, during which the unemployment rate had fallen significantly (a full half of 1 percent, from 4.3 to 3.8 percent), the real average hourly earnings for "production and nonsupervisory" employment—four out of five American jobs—unexpectedly *dipped*: "from May 2017 to May 2018, real average hourly earnings decreased 0.1 percent, seasonally adjusted."[3] Unexceptional, indeed. Workers classified in this way, according to the report, saw their nominal wages inch upward over this period, but not enough to keep pace with inflation. The dip in real hourly wages means that the amount of goods and services workers are able to purchase with a given quantity of money has diminished, slightly but perceptibly. The lowest unemployment rates since the tail-end of the 1990s boom, by most economists' reckoning, should have generated wage increases, as the supply of unemployed workers available to meet growing demand from employers dwindled. But wages fell. The *Washington Post*, reporting the story, asked an economist from Cornell to weigh in: "you would not normally see this kind of thing unless there were some kind of external shock, like a bad hurricane season, but we haven't had that."[4]

The pattern, so confusing to economists, is not new, nor does it date from the crisis period beginning in 2008. Between 2002 and 2012, according to one report published in the midst of the recovery, the "vast majority of wage earners," some 70 percent, had "experienced a lost decade, one where real wages were either flat or in decline."[5] This trend continued over the next five years. Almost all increases in total wages over this period are attributable to salary increases for high-earning, supervisory, or non-production employees.

The appeal to some external force or visitation, be it weather or war, is typical of economists or policy types who cannot square perplexing data with their own simplified schemata. Common sense tells us that when labor markets tighten, wages will rise as employers compete with one another for those workers still seeking work. This inverse correlation between unemployment and wages is so self-evident that most commentators tend to focus instead on an indirect effect of these inevitable wage increases: a sudden surge in inflation. Since labor is a commodity among others, rising costs of labor will drive inflation upward; since labor is also a cost of production, higher wages will be reflected in higher prices for goods and services. And because workers have more income, they will spend more; this will drive demand for consumer goods like televisions and automobiles, forcing up prices for these and other products. But currently, inflation stands well under 3 percent; it has hovered below this threshold, sometimes sinking lower than 1 percent on an annual basis, for the entire "recovery" period since 2009, even as jobs were slowly added.

A Crisis of Worklessness

Not perfect, indeed. How are we to explain these seemingly contradictory phenomena, pairing declining unemployment with stagnant and even falling real hourly wages? One answer is to give in to the tug of doubt we might have about the accuracy of the reported numbers in the first place. The high spirits evinced in the *New York Times*'s celebration of the Labor Department's finding was only a touch dampened by the observation that the rate of "prime-age adults working remains below its historical levels." Other observers are less equivocal: the published figures are just wrong. If the real earning power of most U.S. workers hasn't budged despite the steep decline in those declaring themselves unemployed, it could be because a large number of working-age American adults have stopped looking altogether. The U.S. BLS has in fact recorded a dramatic 6 percent drop (to 62.8 percent in 2016) in the labor participation rate since 1996, with projections for further slippage over the next decade. Closer examination of these statistics reveals that the overwhelming majority of those who have stopped trying to find work are men. In 1996, a full three-quarters of U.S. working-age men were counted as actively participating in the labor market; by 2016, the number was 69 percent and by 2026 could plummet as low as 66.[6]

This widespread withdrawal from the labor market was dictated in no small part by the ravages of the 2008 economic crisis. At their worst, in October 2009, official unemployment statistics reported that one in ten workers was out of work; yet at this point the labor participation rate was 65 percent for the U.S.'s "civilian noninstitutional population."[7] In November

2018, the unemployment rate hit the lowest threshold in a generation, less than 4 percent. But this dip was combined with an even more significant exodus from the labor force altogether, as the participation rate fell to 62.9 percent. Since the U.S. population swelled over this near-decade by 22 million, the "civilian noninstitutional population" grew at a similar rate, by 19 million (from 238 to 257 million). Yet in absolute terms the U.S. only added 9 million jobs, less than one-half the number of new workers added over this period. In a decade, therefore, in which government-supplied unemployment numbers declined precipitously to the lowest level of the new century, no fewer than ten million additional workers found themselves without work.

These data are not hard to find. They are published by the U.S. Department of Labor on a monthly basis. Yet their implications are often hushed up, with economists and political insiders whispering among themselves that the real rate of unemployment is multiples higher than what is reported publicly. The code of silence governing these discussions is broken, though, on occasion. In early 2017, for example, the *Financial Times* soberly noted that the "share of people in their prime years (between twenty-five and fifty-four) who are neither working nor looking for work" stood "at about twenty per cent" (these numbers are substantially higher for younger workers between 16 and 25 and those older than 55). Even if we concede that the published unemployment figures accurately reflect the workless rate for those still seeking work, we can also concur that these data do "not tell us much about the *festering crisis of worklessness in America*."[8]

Explanations for this crisis of worklessness have predictably varied. Some have pointed to the explosion of those receiving disability payments over the past two decades—from 7.7 million in 1996, to 13 million in 2015—as one haven to which workers, unable to find meaningful employment, have fled. Many of those reclassified as disabled might have qualified, before welfare reforms in the 1990s, for other forms of state assistance; workers who once would have been deemed unemployed now carry the stigma of "disability" as they search for jobs, or decide the search is not worth it. The highest rates of disability payments are, predictably, in rural areas from which jobs in manufacturing and mining have fled; four of the five counties with the highest rates of disability are in coal country.[9] Others have focused specifically on the disproportionate number of men that seems to make up this shadow army of the workless. One right-wing commentator, Nicholas Eberstadt, lamenting what he perceives to be the erosion of patriarchal authority in families in which men do not work, echoes the conclusion of the *Financial Times*, speaking both of an "invisible crisis" and, keying his rhetoric high, a "dreadful collapse of work."[10]

To speak of a collapse of work or a crisis of worklessness points in the direction of some objective cause or mechanism responsible for this state of affairs, a fate imposed from without on millions. Eberstadt, in typical arch-conservative fashion, sees this crisis as not simply a social but a "moral" one, in which a shadow army of able-bodied men shirk their familial responsibilities and allow themselves to be dominated by wage-earning women and mothers. But his formulations—decrying men who have "exited the labor force altogether," a "flight from work"—can be given an alternative, and less negative, parsing. Some might strain to hear in these phrases not evidence of a retreat, but the telltale signs of a large-scale exodus from the compulsion to work, or even a refusal of an otherwise objective state of affairs: the unremarked formation of a shadow army that refuses the discipline, constraints, and humiliations of the wages system. Offered a miserable array of poorly paid jobs that require few skills, as stockers, security guards, and hospital orderlies, with little job stability and a truncated work week—perhaps supplemented with off-the-table work for a friend, and minimal state support—it is no wonder that increasingly large numbers of workers turn up missing. If so, still: this withdrawal is no getaway exodus undertaken consciously with friends, families, co-workers, communities; it is silent, atomized, and stigmatizing. For many, this flight leads to an ever-deeper burrowing into the junk culture of the world from which they are otherwise removing themselves: pornography, social media, and video games. And, abject though it is, this lunge for the door remains the austere luxury of men, who tend equally to flee the urgencies of unwaged domestic work.

An especially salient feature of the current crisis is therefore the swelling number of workers who no longer actively take part in the labor market. U.S. labor participation rates are as low in 2018 as they were in 1978, when women were still pouring into the workforce by the tens of millions. Since the actual jobless rate among U.S. workers is therefore much higher than the reported data suggest, it is reasonable to assume that a significant fraction of these ex-workers could, with a change of economic weather, re-enter the workforce; thus even now they exert a virtual downward pressure on the price of labor-power. The looming presence of this shadowy or invisible army of ex-workers would explain the persistence of wage stagnation, despite the apparent tightness of the labor market.

The Slowest Rate in Postwar History

Compelling as it might be, any examination of the conundrum of persistent wage stagnation focusing solely on the supply of and demand for labor leaves out two essential factors determining the price of labor-power. The first is what economists call the labor share of income, the portion of total economic output that is allocated to workers as wages and benefits. Since the labor share of income is inversely proportional to the part of output that returns to capital in the form of profits, any change in the distribution of labor and capital incomes, *assuming the productivity of labor remains constant*, affects both shares, one positively, the other negatively: any rise in wages will come out of the pockets of business owners, and vice versa. Owners of capital will stop at nothing to stymie any attempt, on the part of the organized working class, to bolster its share of income at the expense of their employers. The division of output between wages and profits is the most immediate expression of class power in capitalist economies; it is no surprise that the decomposition of the organized workers' movement over the past fifty years has seen a corresponding erosion of labor's share of economic output. Wage stagnation often means wage suppression: the confiscation of a larger share of output by capital.

The insertion of this class dynamic into the equation is essential, since the owners of capital are highly organized as a social force, and will do everything in their power to extort a larger profit share of income at the expense of labor. But though the consideration of factor shares of income offers a tool for understanding the long-standing leveling out of wages for workers in the u.s., the UK, and elsewhere, attributing the cause of long-standing wage stagnation primarily to wage suppression—the reduction of workers' share of total economic output—misses the second and in fact most decisive factor in the decades-long leveling off of wages: the dramatic tapering off, over the same period, of gains in the productivity of labor. Indeed, the argument made in what remains of this chapter will be that the wage stagnation experienced by workers in countries like the u.s. and the UK is directly tied to these productivity declines.

Fluctuations in the supply of and demand for labor can affect the price of labor in the short term, and within strict limits. As I have already noted, any nominal wage increases that raise business owners' costs of production will either eat into capital's share of income, a relatively exceptional circumstance fought off tooth and nail by those who stand to lose in this equation, or will be canceled by inflation, as rising labor costs are reflected in rising prices of goods and services. What, then, determines wage levels, if not the relative demand for labor exhibited by employers? Or, formulated differently, under what conditions can *real* wages rise (increases that will not be canceled by rising costs across the economy), assuming the division of income between capital and labor remains constant? Only under conditions in which the productivity of labor rises, thereby generating more output per worker (or hour of work). The exceptional successes of the postwar workers' movement, in the U.S. and Europe, which resulted in substantial wage increases over two decades and more, were inextricably tied to unprecedented gains in labor productivity during this same period. In the core industries of the advanced economies, these gains were made possible by the increasing use of automated labor processes in production: the total output per worker in these industries soared, year over year. As productivity rocketed upward, and costs per unit produced declined, the increased margins (assuming, for simplicity's sake, that prices remain constant) could be equally distributed between both parties. In such a scenario, wages *and* profits rise, even as the share of income between capital and labor remains unchanged. In short, assuming the labor share of income remains constant, the only way workers can win increases in purchasing power is to produce more per hour of labor. Rising labor productivity, simplifying greatly for the moment, is possible on the basis of constantly rising ratios of fixed capital per worker, the investment in machinery that makes for expanded productivity. Whence the claim, sung by the chorus of automation "optimists," that—in Paul Mason's words—our epoch promises an "exponential takeoff in productivity."

Where do things stand today with the productivity of labor? And what relationship can be discerned between changes in labor productivity and wage stagnation? The answers are clear enough: wages for workers in once fast-growing economies like those of the U.S. and the UK—indeed, those of most advanced economies across the world—have remained unmoving not so much because an oversupply of labor has driven down its price, but because these economies themselves have remained remarkably torpid. Real wages for workers in the u.s. have been stagnant not simply during the crisis period since 2008; they have remained at roughly the same level for a full forty-plus years, essentially since the middle of the 1970s, during which time demand for labor has fluctuated on a cyclical basis. What accounts for this stagnation throughout the period from roughly 1973 on has been a pronounced slowdown in labor productivity gains.

Never before, we are told over and over again, has the world market been so integrated, if not unified, as with the advent of globalization in the 1990s: offshored manufacturing, just-in-time production techniques, and the computer-aided refinement of logistics can move products cheaply around the world in ever-shorter intervals. By the same token, information and communications technologies, with the aid of vast computer networks and webs of submarine fiber-optic cables, permit exchanges among billions of networked individuals instantly, in real time, by text, phone, or video. Moore's Law means that since 1970 computing power has grown by prodigious leaps, even as the cost of producing it plunges lower. A significant share of retail shopping in the u.s. is now done online, resulting in the creeping obsolescence of the "big box" store, while the logistics and distribution clusters required for the expedited delivery of these goods grow larger and more efficient, and employ more and more workers. The past decade in particular has witnessed a surge in online platforms of all sorts, extended digital markets connecting buyers and sellers of an ever-wider range of goods and services (housing, car rides, temporary work, and so on). The paired Schumpeterian terms "disruption" and "innovation" are relentlessly invoked in news stories and around office coolers, while changes in consumption, especially forms of entertainment, communication, and sociality, have been dramatic and disorienting—even disconcerting—for many.

Nevertheless, statistics collected by departments and ministries of labor tell a very different story. A recent study by the McKinsey Global Institute leads with the observation that "nine years into recovery from the Great Recession [that is, since 2009], labor-productivity-growth rates remain near historic lows across many advanced economies."[11] The recent history of the U.S. economy on this score is remarkable. Since 2007, according to the BLS, the productivity of American workers— the quantity of a given good or service produced per labor hour—has on average risen at an annual rate of only 1.2 percent. Lest we conclude that these numbers have been dragged down by the exceptional circumstances surrounding the recession of 2007 to 2009, it happens that the numbers actually leveled off well into the recovery, and remained in a state of near growthlessness up to the present. For six years, from 2011 to 2017, the following productivity growth figures were recorded: –0.1, 0.8, 0.5, 0.8, 1.3, 0.1, 1.1.[12] This is not all. The 0.75 percent average annual growth rate over the half-decade beginning in 2011 is for *all* sectors of the economy other than agriculture; it includes such typically low-productivity sectors as healthcare, education, restaurants, and so on. If we examine those businesses that have historically made up the economy's most dynamic sector, something stranger is revealed. During that same ten-year interval, what has often been conceived as the literal engine of the economy, the manufacturing sector, exhibited even lower, in fact *negative*, rates of productivity growth: –0.2 percent. From 2011 to 2017, the annual growth rate for manufacturing hovers around this average, when it is not dipping into the red: 0.7, –1.0, 1.4, –0.3, –1.5, –0.2, –0.4.[13] Nothing in this string of subtractions suggests we are in a period of renewal and transformation.

What is even more unsettling about these results is that they cannot be written off as a mere hiccup, a deviation attributable to the undoubtedly severe crisis that began in 2008. If we pan outward from our focus on the past decade or so, a broader trend can be detected. During the period beginning just after the Second World War the core group of Western European and North American market economies experienced a period of unprecedented economic expansion. Those countries with a less-developed industrial base, like Italy and France, saw the productivity of their workers shoot upward at a rate, in the late 1940s, of over 10 percent annually; Spain saw a similar surge in the early 1960s. Both Germany and the UK had predictably more modest but still substantial upticks in productivity during this period. While postwar economic growth assumed Promethean dimensions for these nations, as their industries, beneficiaries of significant private and public investment, raced to catch up with and compete with the American hegemon, the pattern of development—with its concomitant elevation of wages and working-class consumption—continued long after this initial surge, in some cases enduring three decades, to be called variously an "economic miracle," the "glorious thirty years," or simply the Golden Age. While productivity in U.S. industry, already highly capitalized relative to the rest of the world, grew at an impressive rate of 2.6 percent over the course of a quarter-century, from 1950 to 1973, the output per hour of workers in the former Axis powers accelerated even more rapidly over the same period: in Italy, 6.1 percent, and in Germany, just a notch below 7. But it is in Japan that the most impressive feat of catch-up industrialization took place. In a sustained expansion matched only by the Chinese economy after 1990, Japanese manufacturing registered productivity gains averaging a full 10 percent annually for a full quarter-century.[14] By the mid-1960s, these elevated levels of labor productivity made it possible for Japanese and German manufacturers to vie directly with their U.S. counterparts.

Since at least 1973, declining labor productivity has been the rule among all of these beneficiaries of the postwar boom. In the U.S., the downturn began even earlier. The turning point for the American economy was as soon as 1962, after which the inexorable descent began, only relenting for a spell in the 1990s. The BLS figures show that, for the period from 1973 to 1990, U.S. worker productivity rose at an annual rate of roughly 1.3 percent, numbers not much higher than those of this past decade's "recovery." In a perceptive short article written at a particularly grim moment in this recovery, *The Economist* found it useful to set the recent drop in American productivity against a historical tapestry that had been shaking out for "four decades":

> Except for a brief spurt around the turn of the millennium, productivity has grown painfully slowly in rich countries over the last four decades . . . Labour productivity in America fell at a startling 2.2% annual pace in the fourth quarter of 2015; growth of 0.6% for the year as a whole was better, but hardly impressive.[15]

If the falloff in productivity appears particularly relentless in the case of U.S. workers, worse results have been reaped by their peers in Britain. Speaking of the UK's acute case of the so-called "productivity puzzle," Howard Davies, currently Chairman of the Royal Bank of Scotland and at the time Director of the London School of Economics, observed:

> The UK exhibits a particularly chronic case of the syndrome. British productivity was 9% below the OECD average in 2007; by 2015, the gap had widened to 18%. Strikingly, UK productivity per hour is fully 35% below the German level, and 30% below that of the U.S. Even the French could produce the average British worker's output in a week, and still take Friday off.[16]

Historically, and in particular during the exceptional period of postwar expansion, wage rates have tended to move in concert with productivity gains, especially in high-productivity, heavily capitalized sectors (manufacturing, mining, and so on). What was "miraculous" about this three-decade period was not only the prodigious increase in output, productivity, and GDP, but the changes in the texture of the daily life of wage earners in the capitalist world's industrial core (a pattern occurring, unevenly, in China today). Life expectancy rose as access to modern healthcare was made available to most social strata; education levels climbed, while leisure time and activities once reserved for the rich became expectations even among working-class wage-earners. In the era of the postwar peace, real wages rose at an historically unprecedented pace.

The rise in real purchasing power did not, however, mean the aggregate wages distributed to workers could buy a larger *share* of the total output of the economy; working-class wages commanded a larger absolute amount of such goods, but labor's share of income relative to that distributed in the form of profits remained relatively constant through this period. The postwar period was marked, in fact, by an unprecedented institutional environment in which unions and labor federations worked in concert with employers to tie wage increases to productivity gains. This type of contractual framework was often organized at the sectoral and even national level; pacts between employers and unions were arbitrated by the state, which sought to encourage continued economic expansion while discouraging worker distemper and insubordination. A dynamic equilibrium between a rising labor share of income, stimulating consumer demand, and an equally rising profit rate, encouraging capital investment, was targeted: this was the historic compromise hashed out by democratic states in the years after the war. Across Europe in particular, national labor confederations and employers' unions were able to institute a vision of historical advancement, adjusting wages, profit rates, consumption, and investment to ever-evolving conditions of technological "progress": this was the state as planner, seemingly in full mastery of the motions of the business cycle, enlightened mediator between otherwise antagonistic social forces.

"From 1947 to 1973," a recent analysis published by the U.S. BLS notes, "real hourly compensation increased at about the same rate as labor productivity, resulting in a relatively small 0.2-percentage-point gap in growth between these measures over the period."[17] The correlation between growth in real wages and labor productivity implies a constant share of income between capital and labor; had real hourly compensation risen at a lower rate, the labor share of income would have fallen. The stability of this division of income over a quarter-century had its effect on economists' assumptions about market economies. They tended to see, as they were hammering out some of the clichés of their profession as late as the 1950s, the hard-won correlation between wages and productivity not as an orchestrated social artifact, but as a norm: wage levels are dictated not by short-term fluctuations in labor supply, but by more fundamental advances in labor productivity. Over time, this temporary correlation was elevated to the status of stylized fact.

Anwar Shaikh, however, has recently argued that there can be no a priori correlation between the movement of wages and productivity rates. Productivity enhancements establish what he calls the material foundation for wage increases, but their coordination is hardly assured. They moved together, for a time, due to a prevailing balance of power among the actors involved, the forms of organization in place, and a style of governance predicated on the conscious or rational planning of economy understood primarily as a national arena. "Productivity growth," Shaikh writes,

> provides the *material* foundation for a *potential* rise in real wages, and hence for a potential rise in real consumption per worker. But productivity growth does not automatically

lead to growth in real wages. It takes social and institutional mechanisms to create linkages between the two.[18]

In his *Capitalism: Competition, Conflict, Crises*, Shaikh argues that the primary cause of the wage stagnation experienced by u.s. workers since the 1970s was the breaking of the link—historically assured by the vibrant "social institutional mechanism" of the mid-century welfare state—between productivity gains and real wages and a decline in labor's institutional power, as it came under attack by the social forces personified by Ronald Reagan. This attack, which sabotaged the social and institutional mechanisms that held together productivity and real wages in the postwar period, increased the capital share of income and, in Shaikh's telling, restored what had been sagging profit rates, in the 1970s, for owners of capital. Wage suppression resulting in a reduced labor share of income, combined with technological dynamism leading to rising labor productivity, produced a sustained upswing in capital accumulation, coming to an end only with the economic crisis of 2008.[19]

The argument Shaikh puts forward for why real wages for u.s. workers, like those of workers across the advanced industrial economies, have stagnated leaves aside the key feature of capitalist economies I have underlined throughout this chapter: collapsing labor productivity rates. Shaikh isolates *manufacturing* productivity from the productivity of the labor force as a whole. "It is clear," he writes, "that in the early 1980s, beginning with the Reagan-led assault on labor and compounded by foreign competition, u.s. manufacturing workers suffered a remarkable stagnation in real wages, one that continues into the present . . . Real wages of *manufacturing workers* have been stagnant since the 1980s, while productivity has continued to rise."[20] This might very well be true; but since the employment share of workers in manufacturing represents less than one-tenth of the U.S. workforce, and since manufacturing has historically exhibited the largest productivity gains among all sectors of the economy, especially relative to the service sector, which employs four out of five U.S. workers, the evidence Shaikh presents to bolster his argument is misleading.

In addition, there is evidence to suggest that the labor share of income did not decline dramatically until the first decade of the new century. After all, the modest surge in labor productivity in the late 1990s resulted, according to the BLS, in an even more pronounced uptick in the labor share of income. In the first quarter of 2001, the "labor share of output" was as high as 64.3 percent, a level matching that of the second quarter of 1962, and significantly higher than the 61.5 percent registered at the tail-end of the postwar boom, in late 1965.[21] Any explanation of wage stagnation since the mid-1970s, then, would need to take into consideration not simply the changing share of output between capital and labor, but the collapse in labor productivity gains—"the *material* foundation for a *potential* rise in real wages"— that most commentators acknowledge has hobbled the advanced industrial economies of North America, Europe, and Japan since as early as 1973.

The seemingly inexplicable bind in which the advanced capitalist economies find themselves, with insufficient capital investment resulting in collapsing labor productivity, imposes additional limits on the ability of workers to win concessions in the workplace. There are many who, like Shaikh, assign responsibility for stagnant wages to a shift in social power, the dwindling leverage of unions, and the dismantling, in the so-called neoliberal epoch, of the other "social and institutional mechanisms" that once assured labor a stable share of national income. But if the productivity gains that alone afford the "material foundation" for workplace demands are missing, even the most combative worker organizations will run up against forbidding material conditions and limits.

My argument in this chapter has been that only a substantial surge in labor productivity gains provides the material conditions for an increase in real wages for workers, and that the deep, structural reason for wage stagnation over the past four decades in the u.s. and other rich countries has been the absence of such gains. But why have labor productivity gains in these countries fallen off so steeply since the mid-1970s? And what, exactly, do we measure when we speak of labor productivity gains? In the following chapter, I will explore these questions in detail, shifting from the more empirical, data-oriented account I've offered so far toward increasingly theoretical questions.

four

Approaching Zero

As early as 1967, some twenty years before Robert Solow's famous formulation of the productivity paradox, the economist William Baumol offered a persuasive account of why advanced industrial economies tend to exhibit, at a late point in their development, ever-lower productivity growth rates. The key to the riddle haunting today's automation theorists lies, according to his argument, in the fact that such economies are divided into two broad sectors: one he deems technologically "progressive," whose laboring activities and production processes are subject to "innovations, capital accumulation, and economies of large-scale," and a second, technologically "stagnant" sector, consisting of those lines of production whose technological "structure," as he puts it, stymies attempts to raise the productivity growth rates of the labor force employed by it. The argument is as simple as it is, at first glance, paradoxical. It is the very dynamism of the progressive core of the advanced economies that causes the aggregate productivity growth rate of these economies to decline over time. This decline results from two key effects brought about by rapid improvements in production processes in the dynamic sector. The first is that, over time, labor-saving machinery will mean more output is produced with fewer workers; if output remains constant, then by definition such innovations shed workers, who must find employment elsewhere in the economy. The second effect is that the goods produced by the progressive sector will become ever cheaper as efficiencies in the use of labor inputs are found. This means that even if consumers' income remains constant, a smaller share of that income will be spent on these goods, freeing up more income to be spent elsewhere.

Since improvements in the labor process mean the progressive sector is able to produce a given level of output with fewer and fewer workers, more and more labor will be reallocated to the technologically stagnant sector. Because the share of income consumers spend on the goods produced by the progressive sector declines, output in the stagnant sector will rise, since demand for many of the services produced by this sector is income elastic, meaning it rises when more income is available to purchase them. But since labor productivity growth rates remain low in the stagnant sector, rising output will in turn increase demand for labor in this sector. Over the long term, the *difference* in the productivity growth rates between these two sectors tends to grow ever wider, since one sector is continually raising its labor productivity, while in the other labor productivity tends to remain constant. Teachers, in Baumol's account, are no more productive today than they were one hundred years ago, since the labor process they perform resists technological innovation of the sort implemented in, say, an iPhone factory. As a result, the demand for labor will increase in the stagnant sector as output increases; this demand for labor will rise, in turn, at a rate comparable to declining demand for labor in the progressive sector. The process is seamless: the jobs lost in the progressive sector are absorbed by the stagnant one. As more and more labor is reallocated to the low-productivity sector, however, the overall labor productivity growth rate for the work-force as a whole will decline, since any incremental increases in output in an economy with slowing productivity growth will require more and more labor to achieve. Extrapolating this tendency out over the very long term, Baumol's model suggests that under such conditions, that is, a widening gap in the productivity growth rate between the two sectors, "the growth rate of the economy will *asymptotically approach zero*," even though, and precisely because, the progressive core of the economy is so dynamic.[1]

At first glance, Baumol's account offers a convincing account of why the advanced industrial economies of North America, Europe, and Japan have exhibited declining labor productivity growth rates overall, even as their manufacturing sectors have demonstrated growth rates that, while not on a par with those of the postwar decades, typically exceed those exhibited by the ever-expanding service sectors in those same economies. Here is the answer to the so-called "productivity paradox." Solow's contention that he can see "the computer age everywhere but in the productivity statistics" fails to acknowledge that it is precisely the rapid computerization of one sector of the economy that has resulted, paradoxically, in lower productivity growth rates for the economy as a whole.

For the most part, Baumol does not explicitly map his progressive and stagnant sectors onto the more commonly used categories economists employ to divide economies into two broad sectors: the manufacturing and service sectors. This correlation is implicit, however, in his argument. In many labor-intensive services, the quality of a product is determined by the amount of labor required to produce it, as well as the skill level of those performing the service. Teachers are service providers who operate, by contemporary capitalist standards, with a great deal of autonomy in the work place. The unity of the labor process in their case remains relatively intact, immune as it is from the highly differentiated detail division of labor characteristic of capital-intensive industries, like automobile manufacturing. The teacher creates a product—instruction—that requires a relatively low and historically stable teacher-to-student ratio. While this might differ from subject to subject, these conventions are largely invariable and have changed little over the past century, especially in comparison to the rationalizations of the manufacturing and agricultural sectors. Labor processes like teaching are above all resistant to time-saving efficiencies. Any attempt to shorten the time of instruction for a given subject—teaching a class on Chinese history in four months, rather than eight—will almost certainly diminish the quality of the product. An even more direct correlation between quantity and quality can be observed in the case of the masseur, where the quality of the product is inseparable from the time devoted to it. Perhaps more to the point, for our purposes, are the rapidly expanding "care" occupations, be they care of children, the elderly, or the sick. It is these jobs' resistance to time-saving mediations of the technological sort that account for the concentration of new employment in these types of work, since the turn of the century especially.

Teachers not only provide a service whose productivity growth rate is more or less unchanging over time; these services are in turn provided by governments to residents of a city, county, or nation (Baumol's article is concerned, ultimately, with the rising costs of government services: "anatomy of the urban crisis"). The use of this public-sector occupation as an example therefore raises a number of basic conceptual questions that Baumol's own considerations overlook. The first concerns the idea of a "service sector" in its distinction from the manufacturing sector. On what basis are these two sectors distinguished? The second idea concerns the notion of productivity, a concept we have used extensively thus far without interrogating its meaning and its inner contradictions. How, for example, can we compare the productivity of workers who produce products as different as orange juice and haircuts, or classroom instruction and home mortgages? And in what sense can we measure the productivity of a public school teacher, whose "output" is impossible to measure in conventional terms, since it is not sold on the market for money?

The notion of a service sector, like the category of "services" more generally, conceals as much as it clarifies. The more critical pressure is placed on this concept, the less useful it becomes as a tool of analysis. Said to comprise four-fifths of employment in the u.s. and similar high-income countries, the so-called service sector lumps together an enormous number of economic activities that differ in wage- and skill-level, location, size of enterprise, and capital-to-labor ratios. Its definition is largely negative: it seems to include almost any economic activity deemed neither agriculture (farming, but also forestry and fishing), nor industry (manufacturing, but also construction and mining). Importantly, when tabulating the total number of workers designated as belonging to either the manufacturing or service sector, data collectors do not consider individual employees or occupations, but corporations, deeming all employees of a business whose primary product is, for example, manufactured goods as manufacturing employment, even if they are janitors, accountants, legal staff, or computer-repair personnel. This leads to curious anomalies. Apple, one of the largest companies in the world in terms of its market capitalization, is a manufacturing company that owns no factories; only a small fraction of the retail cost of its products, and therefore the source of its profits, is directly derived from their production and assembly by large factories in China and elsewhere. Yet all of its employees—which excludes the much larger number of workers employed by its subcontractors—are characterized, for accounting purposes, as manufacturing-sector employees. From this perspective, the total number of workers reported to be directly involved in manufacturing activity in the u.s. might be *fewer* than even the officially reported dwindling manufacturing share of employment over time reveals. The changing structure of nominally manufacturing firms, which tend to outsource many directly productive activities, and the increasingly misleading frame of "national" accounting practices in a context in which manufacturing supply chains cross continents, borders, and oceans, suggests that the assignment of a particular type of employment to this or that sector of the economy is increasingly tenuous.

But this is not all. Among the almost infinitely varied array of labor processes and products designated "services" by data collectors, there is a deep cleavage between two distinct types of services: so-called business or professional services on the one hand, and consumer or personal services on the other. The former are primarily "intermediate inputs" provided directly to businesses, often manufacturing firms; the latter are sold to individuals or families able to afford them. Among the first we find a wide range of activities, differentiated as much by skill and compensation as they are by concrete labor processes. What, after all, permits workers performing janitorial and legal services, secretaries and designers, to be lumped into the same category of "services"? Almost nothing, save that in each case the activities these employees perform are only indirectly related to the production of material goods. Historically, these tasks were organized "in-house" by large manufacturing firms, rather than contracted out to autonomous firms specializing in them. Over the past forty years or so, capitalist enterprises have tended, in the interests of driving down production costs, to externalize a number of these functions. This leads statisticians who collect these data to assimilate such activities to services, though many of them—research and design are prime examples, but so are trucking and shipping—are part and parcel of an extended manufacturing process. Since 1947, the u.s. economy, like those of the other advanced industrial economies, has witnessed an extraordinary growth in this subsector, as a share of total employment: from a little over 6 to 14 percent of the total labor force.[2] Because of the way employment statistics are reported, however, it is more than likely that a significant portion of this expansion of business and professional services reflects not a change in the proportion of workers performing them, but their reclassification as services rather than manufacturing activities, as more and more companies outsource these particular functions rather than carry them out internally.

The classification of employees as belonging to the manufacturing or service sectors at the scale of the corporation, the subsector, or the nation is therefore highly misleading. Fast-growing subsectors like restaurants, for example, are characterized as "food services," even though their primary activity is the preparation of meals to be consumed by customers; in the fast-food industry, the production of such meals is carried out using highly efficient processes closer to manufacturing, with little to no service component beyond cashiering. If, shifting levels of analysis, we approach this distinction from the perspective of both the concrete labor process performed by individual workers and the nature of the resulting product, the category of "services" is even harder to pin down than first appears.

The term "services" is as old as the study of political economy itself. Adam Smith's pithy definition—a paid economic activity whose product "generally perish[es] in the very instant of [its] performance"—continues to dominate our current understanding of the term. To this idea of services as performances in which the acts of production and consumption coincide ("instant"), Smith opposes those forms of labor that "fix and realize [themselves] in [a] vendible commodity"[3]: a discrete object that can be detached from the body of both the producer and/or the consumer, and be sold or transferred to another owner at a later date. Take the example of a dental hygienist. The labor she performs by definition does not take the form of a "vendible commodity" in Smith's sense: I cannot detach the state of "cleanliness" from my own teeth or body, much less offer this temporary state to a third party.⁴ The material transformation performed by the hygienist is a largely negative one, the removal of detritus rather than the shaping of a given raw material. The often-cited example of the haircut is slightly different: a given material is indeed transformed, yet the resulting "product" is inseparable from the body and person of the consumer. These are clear examples of services, such as they have been defined since Smith. Yet in both of these cases, the occupation is largely an artisanal or craft activity, performed by a single person, with no detail division of labor. In industries with highly articulated labor processes, individual employees are seldom tasked with the production of discrete objects; no single employee, in any case, is wholly or even primarily responsible for the making of a finished good. Each, as the concept of the detail division of labor implies, contributes a small fraction of the labor necessary for its production. Indeed, in many highly capitalized industries like oil refining, where very few employees can be said to be "directly" involved in the handling, shaping, assembling and transport of materials, a worker tasked with simply monitoring or overseeing, perhaps by means of computer-assisted devices, a given production process is said to be engaged in "manufacturing," though he or she has no direct contact with the materials being transformed and very little direct control over the machinery employed.

The emphasis on the complexity of the detail division of labor in contemporary manufacturing and the resulting change in the nature of the concrete labor process inevitably puts into question the distinction between activities directly involved in the production of "vendible commodities" like toaster ovens and iPhones, and what at first glance seem clearly to be mere services with no immediate relationship to the production of use-values. Within every manufacturing firm—assuming the firm so classified actually owns and controls factories, and directly produces manufactured goods—there are any number of staff present on the shop floor tasked with keeping the facilities clean and in working order. Maintenance and janitorial staffs, whether they are employed in-house or supplied by a separate business services company, assure the upkeep and repair of plant and equipment, the smooth functioning of air-conditioning, lighting, and plumbing systems; they are essential to, if not directly a part of, the production process. Not only does their work make possible the properly productive activity of other workers, it can be said to have a significant, if difficult to measure, effect on the labor productivity of those same workers. Richard Walker has argued that these activities should be understood not simply as services adjacent to the production process, but as themselves forms of "indirectly" productive labor, which both "assist" and "augment the productivity of social labor."[5]

Whether at the level of reported statistics—which rely on conventions and methods of data collection that arbitrarily classify companies, entire sectors, and their corresponding labor forces as producing manufactured goods or services, the lumping together of business or professional with personal services— or at the level of concrete labor processes, the catch-all term "services" therefore appears to obscure more than it clarifies. Nevertheless, it is equally clear that those activities usually grouped together under the heading of manufacturing play a special role in industrial economies: together, they make up the most mechanized, the most capital-intensive, and the most "productive" (that is, generate the most "output" per labor hour) sector of the economy. Activities of this sort have historically been associated with industries like automobile manufacturing, steel production, oil refining, and so on. This sector demonstrates a degree of homogeneity—despite the diversity of its products— that stands in clear contrast to the chaos of the economists' so-called service sector. What Baumol calls the technologically progressive sector of the economy is defined historically by the similarity, from firm to firm, and despite the differentiation of output, between labor processes and skill levels, wages, and union footprint: workers are often concentrated in large worksites and often employed by companies that operate at a national or international scale. The "factory," throughout the nineteenth and twentieth centuries, concentrated all these features; but there is no reason why other lines of production, be they in business, professional, or consumer "services," could not assume similar features. There is no reason, at the conceptual level at least, to limit this high-productivity sector of the economy by the types of objects or output produced, or to those that deliver finished products primarily for households rather than intermediate inputs consumed by other private businesses. It is this prospect of more and more types of economic activity being rationalized by means of new, computer-aided, labor-saving machinery that current prognostications of a new automation wave assume.

In reality, the recent trend in the advanced industrial economies has been something else entirely. More and more of the activities performed by workers in these economies seem, instead, to resist improvements that would augment labor productivity, thus forming Baumol's "stagnant" sector. This pattern has puzzled observers for decades now, with few convincing explanations offered for just why the performance of jobs conventionally called "services"—to maintain for the moment a term I have worked hard to dismantle above—generally defies attempts by business owners to fully "subsume" these labor processes, in a manner resembling the rationalization of manufacturing throughout the twentieth century.

A number of conditions, some due to the nature of the concrete labor processes themselves, others peculiar to capitalist economies, conspire to inhibit or prevent the rationalization of a large part of the activities currently carried out by wage-earners. Many of these jobs, like those in education and healthcare, are public-sector employment less subject to the pressures of the marketplace than those in the private sector, where the objective of capturing larger market share often requires businesses to economize on labor so as to cheapen the goods or services they provide. By the same token, many of these services are what economists call non-tradeable, meaning they can only be consumed in proximity to (often in the same place and at the same time as) where they are produced. These labor-intensive services are thus less subject to outsourcing and foreign competition, though there are notable exceptions, particularly in business services (for example, call centers and accounting services for American corporations relocated to India). Despite Baumol's argument that the wages of the progressive and stagnant sectors tend to converge, a substantial number of service employees in the contemporary u.s. economy are poorly paid; low wages, and an ample supply of docile labor, are a fundamental hindrance to the replacement of easily jettisoned precarious workers by fixed capital that requires extensive initial outlays and years to transfer their entire value to the goods and services they supply. Finally, many of these services simply cannot be replaced by machines at all, however intelligent they may be. There are aspects of these performances that, by their very nature, resist the economies and efficiencies promised by mechanization; there is something about their operative structure, their open-ended intuitive uncertainty and complexity, that stymies their replacement by robots. This is particularly the case with so-called personal services, especially those defined as "caring" occupations: jobs that require special attention to the health or well-being of other humans. Sometimes these jobs—one thinks of the hairdresser, or the masseur—require physical activities that combine situational awareness and kinesthetic activities involving subtleties of touch, or ongoing responsiveness to a consumer's response to these actions. Sometimes, in turn, these jobs entail a highly affective charge, which requires a certain level of "skill"—an emotional intelligence—on the part of the laborer that cannot be programmed, a tacit form of knowledge that exceeds the capacity of even the most sophisticated machine-learning systems. This set of barriers to the rationalization of a wide range of activities currently performed by the large majority of workers in advanced economies has created a notable polarization in these economies, between an easily mechanized, capital-intensive, and highly productive sector, and a much larger (in terms of employment share) sector characterized by substantially slower productivity growth.

Just as Baumol's model implicitly relies on the concept of a technologically stagnant service sector defined by the physical or technical nature of both its output and these services' corresponding concrete labor processes, it also relies on a measure of labor-productivity growth whose internal contradictions must be examined in depth before we can proceed further. In fact, labor productivity can be measured in two very distinct and potentially conflicting ways. Baumol, like economists generally, defines labor productivity in strictly value-added terms: the rate of productivity is arrived at by dividing a given firm's output, in money terms, by the amount of labor time required to generate this output. But this notion can be contrasted with a very different measure of labor productivity that defines output not in monetary but in physical units. The first method of measuring productivity conceives of "output" as simply the market price realized by the sale of the goods and services produced by a given entity (a firm, an industry, a nation) minus the market price of the inputs required for their production. The second method takes output and input as physical units of a given product. If we are comparing similar or identical forms of output—this is a point to which I will soon return—this physical or volume measure of output can be useful in gauging the efficiency of different production techniques, or different combinations of labor and machinery. A shirtmaker with a sewing machine is likely to produce more shirts per hour than one who sews by hand. We would be inclined to characterize the more mechanized process as the more productive one, since it generates more physical output per unit of labor time. This "universal" notion of labor productivity is an important one for considering how productivity might be measured in a non- or post-capitalist society, one in which social resources (labor, raw materials, means of production) would be distributed without the benefit of markets and price signals, and with a view not toward the production of profits but the satisfaction of needs.

The relationship *between* these two measures of labor productivity is, however, paradoxical. An increase in the physical or "volume" measure of productivity, under certain circumstances, can result in no measurable increase in productivity formulated in value-added terms (if prices fall more quickly than productivity rises, the net result will be a *decrease* in productivity measured in monetary terms). Because rising labor productivity, understood as physical output per labor hour, means that a given number of units can be produced with less labor and so lower labor costs, the price of these goods will most likely drop; by the same token, the number of units will likely increase, as more efficient companies capture market share from competitors by lowering prices. Imagine a company that is able to lower the price of its shoes by half (from $100 to $50), while doubling the number of pairs of shoes it produces and sells (50,000 to 100,000): in money value, the output would be the same ($5 million). Such a company would, measured in money terms, have exhibited no growth in labor productivity, even as technological changes in its labor process—more units of machinery relative to units of labor—doubled the number of pairs of shoes produced. The same distortion works the other way. If a company belonging to what Baumol calls the technologically stagnant sector generates the same output in physical terms, yet the price per unit surges, the output in money terms will rise. The labor producing that output will be considered more "productive" in value-added terms. In the case of the progressive sector, productivity gains are hidden; in the stagnant sector, gains are attributed where there are none.

Let's complicate things more. Thus far we have understood the measure of labor productivity rates in money terms only for the numerator, that is, the measurable output; the denominator is measured in units of labor *time*. This convention leaves out a key feature of the dynamics of capitalist economies. Business owners are concerned above all with the relation between the value of output and the costs of inputs; for many lines of production, the cost of labor inputs in particular is the most important variable. When we substitute labor costs for labor time, another paradox tied to the use of value terms to measure productivity arises. Suppose a shoe manufacturer wants to raise the total "value" added to the product per labor hour. He or she is confronted with two choices. The first is to raise the physical output per hour, while paying his or her employees the same wages. But as I noted above, rising productivity measured in physical units per hour can be and often is offset by falling price per unit. The second approach is to lower the cost of labor, while maintaining the same output measured in both physical and price terms. This can be done in two ways. The first is to reduce the number of workers, while raising the intensity of labor; the second is to maintain the same number of workers, while lowering wages. In the first case, I have raised productivity by squeezing more output from a given unit of labor, measured in time;[6] in the second case, I have raised the amount of output not in physical terms, but relative to the cost of labor. Though the numerator remains unchanged, the denominator expressed in money terms is smaller; though I have changed neither the labor process itself, by adding new machinery, nor the intensity of labor, I have nevertheless raised the "productivity" of labor by lowering what economists call "unit labor costs." By expressing both output and inputs in money terms, rates of labor productivity can seem to rise with no change in the structure of the labor process itself. Simply by lowering wages—for example, by moving production units to labor markets in which lower labor costs prevail—business owners can increase the productivity of labor as measured in money terms.[7]

A different set of problems arise with the idea that productivity can be measured in terms of physical units. While it is true that within a single sector or line of production such a measure seems possible—the productivity rates between shoe manufacturers can arguably be compared in terms of numbers of shoes made per labor hour—this manner of assessing labor productivity becomes useless the moment we compare rates between sectors. After all, it makes little sense to compare different types of physical output. Shoes don't have much in common with car mufflers, either in terms of their end uses or how they are made. Such comparisons become even more absurd when we equate the production of goods like shoes and mufflers with services like haircuts or used car sales. I can no more use a haircut to run a marathon than I can use my skills as a car salesman to make high-quality mufflers. Considered either from the perspective of their final use, or from the concrete labor processes required to produce different goods and services, there is no way to compare the infinite variety of laboring activities in a given society. And yet in the marketplace these things *are equated* in terms of the money prices they fetch: one pair of shoes might be worth two haircuts, while four haircuts can be worth as much as one muffler. In millions of marketplace transactions, different kinds of product and the particular laboring activities that produced them are compared in money terms. This is why the statistical convention of measuring labor productivity by dividing "output" measured in money terms is the only option available to analysts who want to measure productivity rates between and across different economic sectors producing vastly different physical output.

Nevertheless, measuring output in monetary terms generates still more distortions than those we have tracked thus far. First of all, by restricting its measure of output to those goods and services sold in the marketplace, it effectively excludes from consideration all laboring activities that produce use-values but no exchange-value: activities like childcare and meal preparation performed by families that are necessary for the functioning of the economy as a whole even though, or precisely insofar as, these activities are not exchanged for wages and what these activities produce (prepared food, childcare) are not sold on the market. These activities produce "output" to be consumed, but because this output has no market price it does not, strictly speaking, count as economic output. On the other hand, there are an enormous number of wage-earning activities, almost always defined as "services," primarily performed for the sake not of producing this or that commodity but in order to facilitate the buying and selling of other commodities. These activities can be bought and sold on the market, and therefore have an exchange-value; but they produce no recognize use-value at all. A useful example is the activity of a cashier, who can be said to circulate value insofar as he or she carries out the exchange of money for a product (shoes, a muffler, a haircut). The same can be said for the activity of a security guard, whose job is to ensure that property changes hands only in situations where money is tendered in exchange for it. Though the labor involved has a cost, it is not clear how to measure the productivity of such activities, because the service they provide cannot be considered a directly useful activity in any recognizable sense of the term.

Curiously, financial activity, which in BLS statistics includes related activities like selling real estate and insurance provision, is an example of this problematic type of service productivity. The "output" of a broker working for an investment bank would seem to be the "financial instruments"—equities, mortgages, or derivatives—sold to clients. But these are obligations regarding future commercial transactions, rather than "products" in any normal sense of the word: "Even in concept, there is little clarity about the services that banks provide to customers, much less whether statisticians are correctly measuring those services."[8] It is clear even to observers who do not clearly distinguish between production and circulation activities that the designation of financial sector profits as "value-added" by financial labor is perverse at best. This sector, by definition, merely reallocates existing capital, and is paid a portion of that capital for the function it provides; only in the minds, and methods, of national accounting agencies can such an activity be seen as anything other than an intermediary activity that adds no value to the total social product. To the contrary, the financial sector can best be described as capturing, or appropriating, value that is produced elsewhere in the economy. The boom in financial sector profits over the past three decades in the richest economies suggests not an explosion of productivity in this sector, but that a growing share of the total value produced in the economy as a whole is being redistributed to businesses that perform a range of activities that do not themselves produce value. As Adair Turner notes, more and more of the activities performed by private businesses in the u.s., the uk, and similar economies can be described as *zero-sum distributive functions*. "Numerous jobs fall into [this] category," Turner writes; the array of unproductive operations carried out in mature capitalist economies includes the work of "cyber criminals and the cyber experts employed by companies to repel their attacks; lawyers (both personal and corporate); much of financial trading and asset management; tax accounts and revenue officials; advertising and marketing to build brand X at the expense of brand Y," and so on.[9] We can easily see the absurdity of the notion of measuring the labor productivity of any number of activities currently classified as services. While many service activities, like cutting hair and giving massages, produce goods that are bought and sold on the market, a significant fraction of the activities classified as "services" by economists (including Baumol) produce nothing at all, that is, no use-values at all. Though these services are purchased on the market and those who perform them receive wages in exchange for carrying them out, it makes little sense to measure their productivity.

In conclusion, I want to return to the example Baumol explores: not the financial sector, but teaching. The subtitle of his 1967 article, "anatomy of the urban crisis," spells out the true stakes of his model of unbalanced growth rates between the progressive and stagnant sectors, namely, the budget crises faced by local and regional governments due to the rising cost of social services, traffic planning, policing, and education. According to Baumol, the costs of municipal services rise year after year owing to wage increases for government employees that far exceed their productivity growth rates. How, though, are we to measure the productivity of activities that are carried out in the public sector, rather than by private businesses? Government employees provide services that, like domestic labor performed in private house-holds, are not sold on the market for money; they produce goods without prices. Unlike those who perform unwaged household labor, however, teachers and police officers receive wages in exchange for the services they perform. Since labor productivity rates are typically measured against output measured in money terms, on the basis of the sale of goods or services on the market, government services produce no output, strictly speaking. In order to assess the role these activities play in economic activity as a whole, economists must therefore assign them an "imputed" output, that is, an estimate of the value of these activities had they been sold on the market by private businesses.[10] This convention of assigning economic values to non-market activities suggests that services provided by governments "add" to the total activity of the economy, rather than exist as overhead costs that must be paid out of the total pool of profits generated by the private sector. In fact, because these services are not sold by private businesses, their costs are funded not out of income generated by sales but by tax revenue collected by local, regional, and national governments. These revenues arise not on the basis of economic activity—production and exchange of goods and services—but through the exercise of state authority: the confiscation of a portion of the profits generated by private business across the economy as a whole.

How are we to classify such activities, if they produce no measurable output other than those imputed by economists to measure non-market "exchanges"? In many ways, public services provided by governments are similar to financial services and many retail activities in the private sector, insofar as they do not directly produce value. The activities of a teacher and a banker could not, at first glance, be more different. The first meets a vital need of the community, playing a role in the reproduction of labor-power, while the latter pursues his or her self-interest at the community's expense. The first produces educated people; the second produces nothing at all, apart from arrangements for the transfer of money, though this activity generates its own (substantial) income through the reallocation of capital between borrowers and lenders or investors. Yet both the salaries of public school teachers and the profits of bankers are paid not out of the proceeds of their activities, but through the redistribution of profits generated by the private commodity-producing economy as a whole. Each of these activities, otherwise so different, can be described as types of "unproductive" labor, in a sense that will be explored in the next chapter.

Baumol was correct in seeing that the key dynamic or "differential" governing the world's richest economies is the expansion of such activities—government services, insurance company revenues, management consulting fees, real estate financing and sales, and certain retail activities—relative to value-producing activities, though he impeded understanding of this situation by attempting to analyze it with the economists' concepts of productivity and services. The notion of "services," as we saw, amalgamates a number of activities that perform very different roles in the economy as a whole. Considered from the perspective of whether they produce value, massage parlors and circus performers have more in common with miners and dairy farmers than with police officers and advertising executives. Since productivity can't really be defined for teachers, financiers, and cashiers, they are not intelligibly described as working in a technologically stagnant sector of the economy. It is not, as Baumol thought, the high wages (actually enjoyed by only some members of this category) and low productivity of "service" workers, therefore, that explain the ongoing stagnation of the capitalist economy.

five

Circulation and Control

In Chapter Two, I offered a survey of the broad and decades-long tendency toward slowdown and stagnation characteristic of the advanced economies of North America, Western Europe, and Japan. I paid particular attention to the declining rate of business investment by u.s. companies, particularly since the turn of the century. The period between 2000 and 2003 was uniquely chaotic for the u.s. economy, marked as it was by the collapse of the dotcom bubble in equities markets, wars in Afghanistan and Iraq, and an interest-rate policy that lowered prime borrowing rates—just as the wars were ramping up—to near zero. The ongoing decline in capital spending by private companies was then exacerbated by a decade of economic crisis, beginning in 2008, despite an explosion of borrowing by states, households, and companies alike, as a result of the exceptionally low cost and ready availability of credit. This environment led, I noted, to a pattern of unusual and ominous behaviors within these economies: rising corporate debt levels, both in absolute terms and relative to GDP; the proliferation of so-called zombie firms, getting by on abnormally low debt-service obligations; and a handful of cash-rich, so-called superstar companies, primarily from the "tech" industry, plowing rent-like profits into round after round of stock repurchases, driving up their share prices and market caps for the benefit of shareholders.

I have taken this behavior by the world's leading technology firms to be especially symptomatic of a global dilemma for owners of capital. The decision to use outsized profits to buy back company shares on the open market means these companies found no compelling opportunities for even modest returns on expanded investment in new equipment, buildings, software, or infrastructure: a peculiar situation for companies perceived by most observers as a vanguard of disruptive dynamism and technological innovation.

The drawdown in capital spending by u.s. companies during the crisis was particularly acute, as might be expected during the worst economic downturn since the 1930s. But the trend it reflects is a deeper and long-standing one, beginning much earlier than the last decade. Indeed, a study conducted in the first phase of the crisis (in 2013) outlines just how sustained this downward trajectory has been, noting that, measured as a "share of GDP, business investment has declined by more than three percentage points since 1980." Within this now forty-year-long trend, the decade of the 1990s (primarily its second half) stands out as an exception, during which a host of economic indicators—GDP, labor productivity, business investment—nudged upward, after which the floor appeared to give way again. "It is troubling," the authors write, that over the past decade,

> business investment rates in the United States have stagnated. Between 1980 and 1989, business investment in equipment, software and structures grew by 2.7 percent per year on average and 5.2 percent per year between 1990 and 1999. But between 2000 and 2011 it grew by just 0.5 percent per year — less than a fifth that of the 1980s and less than one tenth that of the 1990s.[1]

There is perhaps no better snapshot of the u.s. economy since the 1970s than this. As capital spending relative to GDP tapered off rapidly over four decades, the brief respite in the 1990s gave rise to the rhetoric of the "new economy," which held that a new round of sustained economic growth would be fueled by the production of "knowledge" and "information." Compared to the prodigious expansion of the capitalist economies of the U.S., Germany, and Japan in the 1950s and 1960s, the gains of the 1990s were modest. The uptick in investment and GDP growth most likely registered a surge in the mechanization— better, "computerization"—of business services in particular: a minor revolution in accounting, inventory, and supply-chain management, fueled by digital technologies first developed in the prior decades.[2] Importantly, no comparable upswing has resulted from the explosion of e-commerce and the proliferation of smart technologies in the past decade. Far from it: *less than one-tenth that of the 1990s.*

Up to this point, I have focused on wage stagnation, unemployment, and labor participation rates, and the secular decline in labor productivity among workers in the world's richest economies. But it is arguably the trend in the rate of business investment that is the most important indicator of the overall health of the economy, for a simple reason: if private businesses are investing in machines and computers, in newer and larger plants and structures, or in research and development, they are doing so in order to raise the productivity of their workers. In periods of expansion, adding more units of capital will be combined with new rounds of hiring; the benefits of this surge in both output and productivity will in turn often be shared with workers, in the form of rising compensation. Inversely, if the rate of capital spending is low, it means that businesses are not expanding, either by acquiring fixed assets or taking on more workers; the result, as we have seen, is a sustained period of wage stagnation, as any marginal increase in productivity growth is distributed to owners of capital in the form of profits. This chain of consequences is intuitively self-evident, since it is only by expanding their productive operations that businesses, and economies, can develop newer, cheaper, and more efficient labor processes, allowing them to raise output, as demand for their cheaper commodities rises. Historically, this logic has been borne out: almost all economic downturns over the past century have been preceded by declining rates of business investment.

Why does the rate of investment decline? As I argued in Chapter Two, companies will not invest in productive operations when they do not expect to receive a worthwhile rate of return on this investment; they will opt instead for the liquidity of cash, often redistributing that cash to investors (in the form of stock repurchases or dividend payments), or pursuing speculative, "zero-sum" opportunities that do not add productive capacity or require hiring additional workers. This formulation, however, suggests that variations in capital spending rates are primarily a result of the psychological disposition ("expectation") of investors, rather than objective limits imposed on capitalists by the business cycle itself. The reason why private businesses reduce investment spending is due, ultimately, to a decline in the average rate of profit across the economy. When profit margins are ample, a larger share of business income can be spent on accumulating fixed capital and, with it, hiring more workers: General Motors can open new factories, with workers to run them. But when profit margins are squeezed, the pool of capital available for investment over and above the costs necessary to maintain current operations shrinks. The rate of profit can therefore be understood as having a crucial regulating role in the performance of capitalist economies, since it determines— that is, puts limits on—the rate of investment and, in turn, the whole series of important indicators I have already discussed: unemployment, productivity, and worker compensation.[3] This makes the explanation for the fall in the average rate of profit across the economy especially important; unfortunately, there is very little consensus among economists about what drives trends in profit rates.

Indeed, there is no prevailing standard by which the profit rate is measured, or even for defining it.[4] Government statistics rely primarily on reporting done by private businesses; profits are generally attributed to any activity conducted by businesses generating returns over costs. While data collected by economists differentiate reported profits at the sectoral level, distinguishing financial profits from those generated by the manufacturing sector, these methods do not register the fact that financial profits, generated through the intermediary services banks and capital markets provide to businesses, are deducted from the profits of value-producing businesses, which must pay lenders for the right to access capital. These difficulties of definition and measurement make published data regarding business profitability unreliable; it is for this reason that the rate of business investment remains the best, if still indirect, indicator of prevailing levels of profit across the economy.

Karl Marx at least has a general theory of the determination of the profit rate, one given plausibility by its success in explaining the course of capitalism's history. Marx's theory is abstract, but the core dynamic it describes can be quickly sketched. By definition, he argues, transforming a given labor process using new technologies will mean that companies will increase the amount of fixed capital they deploy relative to the amount of labor they hire. Sometimes this means these companies can produce the same output with fewer workers; sometimes it means more output is produced with the same number of employees. In certain cases, new technologies will make the goods and services so cheap that demand for them will skyrocket. In this case, output increases dramatically, in turn raising the demand for more labor in a given line of production, despite the introduction of "labor-saving" improvements in the production process. This changing capital-to-labor ratio is called, in Marx's theory, a changing *composition* of capital. Capital investment combines what Marx calls "constant" capital (plant, equipment, raw materials, software, and so on), because these costs reappear in the product, and "variable" capital (the cost of labor-power, or the wage bill). The price of the workers' product that exceeds what it costs to feed, house, and educate them (hence the "variable" character of this element of capital) Marx calls the "surplus value" generated by workers; the relation of surplus value to labor costs Marx calls the rate of exploitation. When the private sector uses investments in technology to increase the productivity of the labor that makes workers' consumption goods, the rate of exploitation increases because the real wage is lowered; this is how productivity increases can enlarge the labor share of product, even while lowering labor costs. Over time, this process, according to Marx, has a tendency to lower the rate of profit, which expresses the relationship between surplus value and total investment, since with less labor expended relative to total capital there is less room for surplus value to be generated. The source of this tension is found in the fact that for Marx—and here his theory departs radically from bourgeois economics[5]—only the consumption of labor-power in the production process generates surplus value, over and above the cost of reproducing this labor-power. As the composition of capital increases across the economy as a whole, that part of the production activities performed by human laborers dwindles, relative to the total expenditures made by private businesses.

Marx speaks of a *tendency* for the rate of profit to fall because the general law he posits—investment in labor-saving technology means capital stock grows more quickly than investment in labor-power—is offset by countervailing factors. Three in particular are relevant for our purposes, one immanent to the process of rising capital composition, the other two forced on labor by capital if the relations of force in the workplace permit them. In the first case, the rising ratio of constant to variable capital, denominated not in physical but in value terms, is offset because of the cheapening of constant capital: an expected effect of rising labor productivity, after all. If the productivity of the labor that produces machines or raw materials rises precipitously enough, the cost of capital as a whole, against which profits are measured, will increase more slowly, slowing in turn the fall in the profit rate. (In Marx's terminology, this is a case in which the "value" composition of capital does not rise in step with its "technical" composition.[6]) This "endogenous" check on rising capital composition should be distinguished from another, much different counter-tendency: as profitability falls, the capitalist class will understandably force lower wages on workers and, alternatively or in combination with this, "sweat" more output out of a given quantity of labor, by speeding up or otherwise intensifying the labor process (thereby raising "productivity" without additional labor-saving machinery). In the first case, wage suppression, capitalists raise the rate of profit simply by lowering their labor costs; in the second case, they raise output per paid labor hour not through modernizing a given production process but through disciplining their workforce more frequently.[7]

The technique of sweating labor requires, in most cases, an increase in the number of supervisory personnel to oversee the labor process and enforce these new requirements. In the third volume of *Capital*, Marx underlines that the labor of supervision is a special category of labor: it performs the function of directing and overseeing the labor process, disciplining the workforce, and ensuring the most efficient use of the labor-power hired by business owners. Supervisory labor is not carried out by business owners themselves, save in cases of small-scale production, but is delegated to a special class of employees. This type of labor is a necessary feature of productive activity in any society in which the vast majority of workers do not control their productive instruments and raw materials and must therefore work for those who do, conditions which prevail as much in ancient and modern slavery systems as in capitalist societies. The "work of supervision," Marx writes, "necessarily arises in all modes of production that are based on opposition between the worker as director producer and the proprietor of the means of production. The greater this opposition, the greater the role this supervision plays."[8] What is specific about the supervisory function in the case of capitalist social relations is that it ensures that the labor-power purchased on the market and consumed in the labor process produces more value than is necessary for the reproduction of that labor-power, whose value is represented in money form as wages. During periods of stagnation and crisis, when sagging profit rates prevent business owners from raising labor productivity by adding more or newer units of fixed capital, this type of labor assumes a special mandate: the discipline it administers in the workplace is often the sole means of raising productivity under such conditions. Given the heightened importance of this disciplining function in economic downturns, we can even expect—paradoxically—the ratio of managerial staff to non-supervisory employees to rise during turbulent periods.

Supervisory labor is characterized by Marx as one of two primary categories of what he calls (reshaping a terminology taken over from classical political economy) "unproductive" labor, with what he calls "circulation" labor representing the second type. In the first case, as we have seen, the labor performed is necessary to ensure that the labor-power capitalists purchase in exchange for wages is used in such a way that it produces a quantity of value over and above the costs of its replacement; that is, it is necessary for the production of surplus value. Yet supervisory labor—insofar as it does not directly participate in, but only organizes and oversees, the labor process—does not itself generate value or surplus value. It generates neither the value necessary to reproduce its own labor-power, nor the surplus value that is appropriated by capitalists in the form of profits. It is a necessary but "incidental" cost of carrying out capitalist operations that must be paid for out of the profits earned elsewhere in a given firm or in the economy as a whole.

Circulation labor performs very different functions. Where, in Marx's understanding of capitalism, supervisory labor is a structural feature of the capital–labor relation in the sphere of production, the labor of circulation—as the name suggests—performs a wide range of activities required for the "realization" of value, its formal conversion from commodity to money. The labor of circulation includes what we earlier identified as the "service" activities necessary for the buying and selling of goods, covering almost every moment in the capitalist valorization process between the end of the production process and the transfer of ownership from producer to consumer: accounting and legal counsel, cashiering and warehousing, security and insurance services. This category can be extended to those activities that specialize in capital allocation ("financial services") as well, facilitating or financing the operations of industrial capitalists. The shrinking industrial base of the advanced capitalist economies, combined with and occasioned by prodigious increases in both output and labor productivity in this sector since the Second World War, has meant a dramatically changing composition of the workforce in these countries, as more and more labor is allocated to circulation and, to a lesser extent, managerial activities.

In fact, this reallocation of labor is a key to understanding what we discussed in earlier chapters as a rapidly expanding service sector, now making up as much as 80 percent of employment in the u.s. and the uk. Given the confused nature of the concept of "services" as used by economists, this situation is better described as a shift of a larger and larger share of labor activities toward "unproductive" activities, be they activities of circulation or supervisory and managerial functions that ensure the efficient use of labor, materials, and machinery. In Marx's terms, these activities are unproductive: they do not produce a product, whether good or service, that can be sold for a profit. While a masseuse working for a massage parlor produces massages that cost more than her labor costs, and hence a profit for her employer, a security guard merely ensures that a certain property remains private; both his labor and the security firm's profits are paid for out of profits generated at the enterprise he guards. In the same way, financial and retail activities are unproductive, as are activities that produce goods and services but are not sold on the market, such as household production and government services. From Marx's point of view, "productivity" in capitalism properly refers to the production of value and surplus value; an increase in supervisory and circulation labor means a decline in the amount of labor consumed productively and so capable of generating profits for business owners.

Marx's approach allows us to understand that the rising proportion of the labor force working in circulation and supervision represents an increasing cost to the system as a whole. This introduces an added complication to Marx's theory of the tendency for the average profit rate to fall. What if a significant portion of the wage bill includes personnel who perform activities that do not produce value, as is the case with circulation and supervisory labor? Since these workers do not produce surplus value or, a fortiori, sufficient value to provide for their own reproduction, their wages must be paid out of surplus value produced by productive workers elsewhere in the economy, thereby drawing down the total surplus value available to capitalists for new investments. Since profits must be shared between productive and unproductive enterprises, the rising ratio of unproductive to productive labor represents an additional downward pressure on the profit rate. The increasing productivity of labor, in Marx's sense of a rising rate of exploitation, must therefore compensate not only for the reduction in the total demand for labor relative to the capital mobilized, but for the increasing costs of circulation and supervision, as more and more labor is allocated to non-productive activity.

But why do the costs of circulation and managerial labor increase? Aren't they just as susceptible to labor-saving innovations as productive activities such as those in industries like manufacturing, mining, and agriculture? This is, of course, the basis of today's forecasts of the dire effects of automation on service-sector employment. In an important commentary on this question formulated forty years ago, Paul Mattick underlined the growing "disproportion" between labor allocated to productive activities and to those representing costs of circulation. The increase in these costs is

> a consequence of the increasing productivity of labor, for the growing mass of commodities, produced with less and less labor, requires a disproportionate increase of the labor employed in distribution. This disproportionality has its source, on the one hand, in the enlargement and extension of the market and, on the other hand, in the *as yet unresolved fact* that the increase of productivity in the distribution process proceeds at a slower pace than in the production process . . . The slower advance in the productivity of the so-called service sector of the economy depresses the rate of profit.[9]

Mattick's argument here recalls that of William Baumol discussed in the previous chapter. In both cases, what is essential is a conception of the economy as divided between two sectors, one subject to ongoing and rapid labor-productivity increases, the other defined by a "slower advance" in the deployment of labor-saving technologies. Where Mattick's argument departs radically from Baumol's is in his characterization of the technologically stagnant sector not as a service sector ("so-called service sector"), but as a sector defined by activities that do not produce value or surplus value. These activities may also in many cases be services, such as they are defined by mainstream economics. But this fact is of no significance, as we argued in the previous chapter. What is decisive is whether an activity produces more value than the wages paid to perform it, or whether it does not. This distinction has no essential connection with the physical labor process these activities require. Whether a given type of labor is productive or not therefore depends instead on what role it plays in the total circuit of capital. Mattick's argument emphasizes the fact that as capitalist economies produce larger amounts of goods and services, more labor must be consumed by private businesses that do not directly produce value. The two most important types of activity are supervisory and circulation labor. Since these activities are by definition unproductive, they are a cost to capital, rather than a source of new value; they are paid for out of the profits other productive businesses generate, rather than producing profit themselves.

The growing disproportion in the allocation of labor between value- and surplus-value-producing activities and those that merely facilitate the realization of value incorporated in commodities in the marketplace is due to the widening gap between labor productivity gains in the immediate production process, on the one hand, and those in "the distribution process," on the other. The only way to overcome the problem of the cost to capital of this ever-worsening imbalance between the technologically progressive industries and slow advances in the so-called service sector is, Mattick argues, an even greater disparity between these two rates of labor productivity growth. It is only by means of still "further increase[s] of the productivity of labor in general and that of productive labor in particular," that is, through ramping up the rate of exploitation in the immediate production process, that the swelling costs of circulation (and, implicitly, supervision) can be offset.

These formulations nevertheless beg the question: why do labor productivity increases in the distribution process (or the so-called service sector) proceed at a slower rate than those in the productive segment of capital's circuit? Why wouldn't the antidote to the growing disproportion in allocation between productive and unproductive labor be found in accelerating the productivity gains of circulation and supervisory labor directly, primarily through automating them? Mattick speaks in this passage of an "as yet unresolved fact," as if the disproportion were not a structural feature of capital accumulation but a contingency that might be overcome in the future. But he also suggests that the limits to raising the productivity of workers tasked with circulating value in particular reflect a crucial change in the relation between production activities and the distribution process. "Whereas the production process becomes increasingly more centralized into fewer and bigger enterprises," he writes, "the distribution process is increasingly 'decentralized.'" Here, the laws of motion regulating the accumulation of capital are elaborated in terms Marx only left implicit: if productive activities tend to be concentrated and centralized in fewer and larger firms, distribution activities are by necessity dispersed in space, and carried out in a large number of, by definition, smaller workplaces, at least relative to those companies focused on productive activities. This phenomenon is particularly clear if we consider a typical consumer good, like air conditioners. Today, over 80 percent of the world's climate-control devices are produced in China; one in three residential air conditioners are produced by a single Chinese company (Gree). Yet despite the growing demand for residential air conditioning in mainland China, a much larger percentage of this output is consumed in North America, a process involving extensive shipping networks and small, spatially dispersed retail outlets staffed by a large number of low-wage sales personnel. This pattern, in which enormous productive gains captured through economies of scale at the point of production are offset by more labor-intensive activities in the circulation process, appears to be a structural feature of global capitalist production.[10]

Mattick's emphasis on the rising ratio of unproductive to productive labor and its effect on the average profit rate for mature capitalist economies was later picked up by the Marxist economist Fred Moseley, first in his *The Falling Rate of Profit in the Postwar United States Economy*, published in 1991, and later in a more speculative essay from the same decade on the "Rate of Profit and the Future of Capitalism." In the later essay, Moseley attempted to puzzle out what he took to be an apparent anomaly in the performance of the u.s. economy since the 1970s. Writing in the midst of the small economic boom of the late 1990s, Moseley noted that rising labor productivity gains since the 1970s, combined with stagnant real wages, should have resulted in a "significant increase in the rate of profit." Yet the rate of profit continued to decline, according to his own measurements, despite a concerted campaign of wage suppression combined with modest increases in labor productivity. In the language of mainstream economics, rising labor productivity, combined with stagnant wages, should result in a growing capital share of income, as all benefits of economic growth are distributed in the form of larger profits. In Marxist categories, rising labor productivity, combined with a campaign of wage suppression, should raise the rate of exploitation; if this rate of exploitation rises more quickly than the rate at which the composition of capital increases, then the profit rate on average should rise in its turn. In our earlier discussion of the countervailing tendencies that check the decline in profit rates, we singled out three: declining costs of constant capital, wage suppression, and rising productivity rates due to "squeezing" labor. Moseley notes that though all of these features were present in the period he is analyzing, from roughly 1980 on, the trending decline in profitability was not reversed. Why? Because this period saw a "very significant increase in the ratio of unproductive labor to productive labor in the postwar U.S. economy."[11]

Here we circle back to the argument first proposed by Mattick: the declining profit rate in the U.S. economy since the 1970s is attributable not simply to the rising organic composition of capital, but to the growing disparity in labor productivity growth between two "sectors" of the economy, one productive of value and surplus value, the other not. Moseley explains that disparity in this way: "The main cause of the relative increase of unproductive labor was the slower 'productivity' growth of circulation labor compared to productive labor, which seems to be due to the inherent difficulties of mechanizing the functions of buying and selling, which must remain to a large extent person-to-person transactions."[12]

Moseley leaves aside the growing ratio of managerial to non-supervisory labor as a relatively minor part of the picture: such labor makes up a mere fifth of the workforce deemed "unproductive." Nevertheless, Moseley's enumeration of the various circulation activities that constitute the bulk of unproductive labor in advanced economies focuses too tightly on the act of monetary exchange. Circulation, after all, includes functions such as legal representation, insurance coverage, janitorial, security, and maintenance services, sales and marketing, and—particularly important for today's "just-in-time" supply chains—warehousing and certain types of transportation.[13] In principle, the growing output of an expanding economy will require a larger number of workers to ship, store, insure, guard, buy, and sell this mounting accumulation of goods and services. There is no a priori reason why this number should rise relative to that of production workers, however. Provided that productivity in each sector grows at comparable rates, the ratio of production to circulation labor could remain unchanged, even as output expands. Why, then, has "the 'productivity' of circulation labor increased more slowly than the productivity of productive labor"? The primary cause of the difference in rates of productivity is due to the "inherent difficulties" of mechanizing, or automating, the labor performed in the "circulation" segment of the capital circuit: primarily because these activities "*must* remain to a large extent person-to-person transactions."[14]

Moseley turns to the automobile industry—as a moment ago I turned to the production and sale of residential air conditioners—in order to clarify this logic. While the productivity of workers tasked with making automobiles has risen steadily since the end of the Second World War, abetted by a wave of automation beginning in the mid-1950s, very few improvements or labor-saving efficiencies have been found for the selling of these same automobiles, which are still shipped by the many thousands to dealerships across the country to be sold by automobile sales-persons. These person-to-person transactions have yet to be replaced by online and automated processes, by which cars could be purchased directly from the manufacturer and shipped to consumers, with no need for expensive circulation overhead like automobile dealerships and sales staff. Consumers still find it necessary to inspect, and often test-drive, these vehicles in person; and because dealerships (in the U.S. at least) are often franchises which compete against one another, salespersons are necessary to negotiate final sales prices based on wholesale prices and available inventory, among other considerations.

Ten years after Robert Solow famously declared he could find computers everywhere but in the productivity statistics, Moseley contended that "computer technology" broadly understood—in 1998 the Internet, cellphones, and computer networks as we now know them hardly existed—might reverse the trend toward higher unproductivity-to-productivity ratios in the composition of the U.S. workforce and thereby restore a profit rate that had been sagging already for three decades. "New computer technology is being applied to many of the unproductive functions of circulation (accounting, billing, check processing, cashiering, etc.)," Moseley observed in 1998, and "this new technology has reduced and will probably continue to reduce the need for circulation labor." These lines, a version of the technological "lag" narrative I discussed in an earlier chapter, were written as the U.S. retail giant Wal-Mart had been developing, for a decade or more, efficiencies in supply chain and inventory management through the exploitation of economies of scale and the innovative use of tracking devices such as UPC barcode technologies and, later, radio-frequency identification tags. The explosion of online retail remained over a decade away. Social media companies like Facebook and Twitter did not exist. Google would not register its domain name until September 1997; Amazon's initial public offering occurred in May of the same year. From the perspective of the contemporary mediascape— the integration of cellular phones, social media, streaming video, often in a single "screen" or device—Moseley's prediction of further important developments in "computer technology" seems to hit the mark. But so does his conclusion (now, a quartercentury later) that the adoption of these devices by private business "has not yet been strong enough to fully eliminate the relative increase of circulation labor": despite the proliferation of e-commerce capabilities and the ubiquity of highly calibrated, algorithmically regulated advertising, there is little evidence that labor productivity gains in the sphere of circulation have been particularly prodigious.[15]

In fact, despite the ubiquity of online commerce in the everyday life of U.S. consumers, today only one in ten sales transactions take place "automatically" and remotely, rather than in those "person-to-person" exchanges that remain so essential for commercial activity in otherwise technologically saturated societies. The story is somewhat different in China, where up to a third of sales are carried out by means of automated online tellers. Even so, the Chinese economy continues to add millions and millions of service jobs year after year: this sector of the Chinese workforce is growing in absolute terms as well as relative to manufacturing employment. We have reason to believe that the most spectacular gains in labor productivity in the sphere of circulation would be offset by the growing number of workers required to transport, store, guard, sort, and deliver items ordered online, without the aid of a "person-to-person" transaction. The labor once performed by consumers—driving or walking to a retail outlet to acquire consumer goods—requires, in the online shopping model, paid delivery persons, not to mention the overhead of constant capital represented by a fleet of trucks and fuel, or the array of additional people required to maintain them (hence the still sporadic outsourcing of delivery operations to non-employees who use their own vehicle).

Rather than focusing entirely on the circulation process, we should instead look closely at the way in which automation is affecting that other primary form of unproductive labor: supervisory activities. An important trend in contemporary capitalism is the use of computer technology or "automation" to augment or replace not the large masses of circulation labor currently required but the much smaller yet perhaps even more vital function of supervising and controlling the labor process itself, on behalf of business owners. The automation of managers and supervisors, or of supervisory functions, can be seen in a number of key segments of the total circuit of capital. These functions, when they employ human labor, are not directly value-adding, and are paid out of surplus value captured in the immediate production process; yet because the express purpose of these agents is to extract as much "productivity" from a given mass of labor as possible, their activity—raising the productivity of others—cancels, at least in part, the drag their own function effects on profit rates. In most cases, managerial labor is less exploited labor than a labor of exploitation; this labor often consists in squeezing or "sweating" additional activity out of a given labor hour, whether through speeding up the labor process as a whole or by plugging the "pores" (bathroom and lunch breaks, and so on) of the working day. The labor historian Kim Moody has underlined the way the just-in-time philosophy of production, with its globe-traversing supply chains and complex logistics technologies, has relied extensively on the intensification of work for employees all along the extended production sequence, utilizing "electronic and biometric forms of work measurement and monitoring" to exert these pressures.[16]

Indeed, one of the great breakthroughs in the application of labor-saving devices in workplaces along these chains—from Chinese factories to warehouses and retail outlets in the u.s. and Europe—has been the increasing automation of supervisory rather than low-paid circulation labor. Here we have the worst of both worlds: low-tech manual labor presided over by all-seeing, "tracking" eyes and ears. In January 2018, Amazon patented two wearable devices to promote the efficiency of its warehouse employees; worn on wristbands, these devices "would use ultrasonic pulses—pitches too high for human ears to detect—to connect with inventory modules on bins to track a worker's hands. Vibrations would communicate information to the wearer, such as alerting someone when they put something in the wrong bin."[17] Uber has been shown to collect enormous amounts of data on its drivers, even when they are not "at work." And in China, rapid advances in "ai-aided surveillance," in particular facial recognition technology, are increasingly being used "on construction sites, enabling managers to track how many hours workers are on site and who is slacking"; "smart sunglasses," used primarily by police to monitor civilians in train stations, are now being supplied to "manufacturing plants for use in time management and quality control."[18] The great virtue of these technologies, from the perspective of state authorities and owners of capital, is their flexibility: they can be easily adapted from techniques of crowd surveillance and control to workplace monitoring of individual employees or work units, observing and measuring performance from minute to minute.

But the nightmarish near-future of an AI-aided "surveillance state"—or better yet, a "smart city"—can wait. Sometimes all it takes to compel more productivity from a given group of workers is a near-depression of the sort experienced in the U.S. and Europe over the past decade: that is, the very decade in which the promises and threats of automation have been promoted with such fervor. Late in Martin Ford's *Rise of the Robots*, the author puts his finger on a peculiar inversion characteristic of the "Great Recession of 2007–09." Rather than the expected pattern of declining productivity as output falls while workers hold on, tenuously, to their jobs, in the severity of the crisis environment, "productivity actually increased." Ford explains:

> Output fell substantially, but hours worked fell even more as businesses very aggressively slashed their workforces, increasing the burden on the remaining workers. The workers who kept their jobs (who certainly feared more cuts in the future) probably worked harder and reduced any time they spent on activities not directly related to their work; the result was an increase in productivity.

If an economic boom can be defined as rising productivity combined with even more rapidly rising output—thus drawing in rather than shedding workers—the scenario that played out between 2007 and 2009 represented the inverted image of a boom: output fell, but the workplace downsized even more rapidly, resulting in an uptick in productivity despite these precipitous declines. What stands out about this particular form of productivity increase is that it was won—if that is the word—not through the addition of labor-saving equipment or machinery, but through the threat of termination. The prospect of being out of work has always served as a disciplinary device for employees. But during the Great Recession, when workers witnessed their colleagues sacked as businesses saw demand for their products dry up and bank financing disappear, the net effect of the threat of termination was a temporary bump in output per hour: more labor was squeezed from the same mass of labor time.

Lest we imagine these patterns to be those of a cyclical, if atypically severe, downturn, a 2014 study by a group of researchers at MIT detected a similar, long-standing trend in the post-dotcom era, even in industries that incorporate relatively high levels of information technology. Referring specifically to Brynjolfsson and McAffee's ubiquitous *Second Machine Age*, whose core claim it summarizes as "U.S. workplaces have been, and will continue to be, automated and transformed by information technology (IT) capital," these scholars concluded, to the contrary, that "there is . . . little evidence of faster productivity growth in IT-intensive industries after the late 1990s." When this evidence did surface, however, its origins were traced not to an uptick in capital-to-labor ratios thanks to new IT and automation technologies implemented in the aftermath of the tech boom in the second half of the 1990s, but to "declining relative output accompanied by even more rapid declines in employment." Where Ford detected an inversion in the normal recession-years pattern in 2007–9—labor productivity increased rather than fell—the MIT study by Daron Acemoglu and others found that this toxic combination of declining output and even more precipitous job losses was not only typical of the entire post-dotcom epoch (from 1999 on), but was even occurring in computer-rich firms in the manufacturing sector, rather than among typically low-productivity service sector businesses. But where the economists at MIT did not speculate on the working conditions, the relations between employers and the workforce, that make such ephemeral gains possible, Ford ventured an explanation that can be backdated to before the onset of the crisis, to the turn of the century. If productivity gains have been won, it has not been through a revolution in the design of work flows, the replacement of humans by machines, or advances in automation. The true "advances," such as they are, have been in the domination of the labor process by employers: their ability to coerce more labor out of a given hour by means of refinements in supervision, oversight, and workplace discipline.

six

The Servant Economy

Compared to previous employment booms, which were caused by the rapid growth of the most-productive enterprises, the experience of the past quarter-century suggests the growth of make-work has been the main thing preventing mass joblessness.

—MATTHEW C. KLEIN

In December 2015 the U.S. BLS issued a news bulletin with a set of next-decade employment projections for the U.S. labor market. At the time, the U.S. economy was in the midst of an especially sluggish recovery from the global recession that began in 2008. Though the recession had been declared over by mid-2009, six years later there was little sign of the spirited rebound many observers expected or hoped for. The U.S. economy exhibited little growth in the way of GDP or labor productivity, and wages continued their decades-long pattern of stagnation. The sole bright spot, it seemed, was the reduction in the published jobless rate, which had reached a full 10 percent by October 2009, the second highest level since the beginning of the Cold War; by the end of 2015, it had been cut in half.[1] In concrete terms, this meant that over six years, more than 11 million workers found jobs.

What kinds of jobs were they? In an earlier set of projections covering 2004 to 2014, the BLS anticipated that retail sales positions, along with jobs like customer service representative, janitors, waitresses and "combined food preparation and servers" and home health aides and "nurses aides and orderlies" would be among the "occupations with the largest projected job growth."[2] All indications are that, despite the intervention of the worst economic crisis since the Great Depression at the dead center of the decade in question, these projections were largely on target. One report from 2017 noted that four of the top five occupations with the most growth since the recession were in food and beverage preparation and serving, on the one hand, and in personal care and service occupations, on the other, to the tune of 6.5 million jobs; these jobs all brought in less than $25,000 a year, well below the median. Meanwhile, the largest job losses were in mid-level clerical work, with substantial hemorrhaging in office and administrative support positions like secretaries, administrative assistants, and bookkeepers. All told, three out of four jobs added during this period earned below the median wage.[3] The declining unemployment rate was heralded by the political class as reassuring news, a sign that order was being restored in the economy. Putting people back to work meant, in these crisis years, that millions now found themselves making and serving food in restaurants and bars—for most, fast food—or, in the case of personal care aides, tending to the needs of "clients," whether these be "light cleaning, cooking, running errands, and doing laundry," or "assisting them with bathing, showering, grooming, and other personal hygiene tasks."[4]

So where do things stand now, with the u.s. economy almost ten years into the recovery that began in mid-2009, with published unemployment figures as low as 3.5 percent (as of February 2020)? Extending forward all the way to 2024, the most recent bls job market projections track closely to the pattern projected in 2004. Consistent with even longer-term trends, almost the entirety of net job growth in the u.s. over this period—nineteen of every twenty new jobs—is expected to be in the broad "service" sector, a motley collection of occupations and labor processes that already make up over 80 percent of employment in most of the world's advanced economies. Significantly, some 40 percent of job growth will be in the so-called healthcare sector, a category that brings together medical services and those delivering "social assistance," which can mean anything from child daycare to emergency relief services and vocational rehabilitation. This new spurt of growth will make the healthcare sector the largest in the U.S. by 2024, surpassing both the business services and government sectors. By the same token, the share of GDP to be spent on healthcare will break 20 percent, compared to just 12 percent in 1990.[5] This general reallocation of labor capacity toward "healthcare" is reflected in the BLS bulletin's report on those specific lines of work expected to grow most quickly. The three occupations expected to add the most positions over the decade all belong to the medical profession, specifically (and in order) personal care aides, registered nurses, and home health aides.[6] Expanding the list to twelve, we can add medical assistants and nursing assistants. What is telling about this group of occupations is that only one of them requires as much as a bachelor's degree and is deemed a form of "skilled labor"; two require a mere certificate, while the final two require "no formal education" at all. Four of the five positions earn less than $30,000 a year.

But this doesn't tell the whole, sobering, story. Of the top eight jobs in the list, which add occupations in retail sales, restaurants, customer service, and janitorial services to those in healthcare, seven require less than a bachelor's degree, and, other than registered nurses, none earns more than $31,000 a year. These seven occupations alone, all of them low-wage, low-skill service occupations despite their classification among different sectors of the economy, are projected to add well over

2 million jobs over the full decade, close to 22 percent of the total number of new jobs.[7]

    While the trend we are tracking has accelerated in the period since the crisis struck in 2008, recent research has concluded both that this pattern was established decades earlier, and that it is a feature not only of the u.s. economy but of a large group of European countries—among the most "advanced" economies in the world—as well. In a 2013 paper, MIT economists David Autor and David Dorn demonstrate that after a three-decade period following the Second World War, during which growth in so-called service occupations remained flat or declined, jobs classified as belonging to the "the lowest skill quartile expanded sharply" between 1980 and 2005, with their share of u.s. labor hours growing a full 30 percent over those two and a half decades.[8] The authors define service occupations as those kinds of service sector employment which deliver "personal services" that are "among the least educated and lowest paid categories of employment," and which can range from "food service workers, security guards, janitors and gardeners, cleaners, [and] home health aides" to "child care workers, hairdressers and beauticians, and recreation occupations": in short, the very group of occupations, and a few others, that the BLS has identified as primed for still another expansion, well into the next decade. To put this explosion in low-wage, low-skill personal services in perspective, the projected number of new jobs in the u.s. economy classified as security, healthcare support, food preparation, janitorial and grounds maintenance, and "personal care" occupations is expected to reach 3 million; in contrast, so-called "production occupations" (woodworkers, bakers, metalworkers, quality control inspectors, and so on) will most likely lose close to 300,000 jobs, while the transportation and materials-moving group, comprising everything from truck and delivery drivers to warehouse employees—what has been called the fast-growing logistics sector, in an era dominated by offshoring and e-commerce—will add fewer than 500,000 workers. This beefing up of employment in the sphere of "logistics" more than makes up for the loss of employment in the productive core. But the growth in jobs in circulation will be quickly outstripped by the selected group of service occupations I cite above. For every job added in what labor historian Kim Moody highlights as a burgeoning and factory-like logistics subsector, six workers will find themselves serving food, cleaning floors, watching children, or giving baths.

But just why have the wealthiest nations and their economies seen such a proliferation of low-income, low-skilled jobs made up of what David Autor calls "manual task-intensive operations" over the past three or four decades, and especially since 2008? Autor fingers the progressive automation of a wide range of labor-intensive operations in the so-called "middle" of the labor market over this period as responsible for the current surge in jobs at the bottom of the wage-scale. Where in earlier epochs of technical change it was jobs in agriculture, then in industry (manufacturing, mining, and so on), that were primarily affected by breakthroughs in replicating repetitive labor processes, recent innovations have beset administrative, clerical, and "office" work in turn. Any white-collar job structured around routine or predictable tasks, especially those comprised primarily of managing and transforming information, has become vulnerable to replacement.

Here, though, we must be careful not to confuse jobs or occupations with tasks. What a particular occupation "does" is never one thing. A job is only ever a specific grouping of discrete tasks, some of which are more repetitive and easily mimicked by machines, others of which are more intuitive, subjective, contingent. Automation replaces tasks, not jobs. When the principles of automation are introduced into a particular branch of production, this tends to compel a restructuring of the prevailing division of labor rather than simply suppressing this or that "occupation." The fate of the bank teller is a well-known example. The introduction of the now-ubiquitous automated teller machine (ATM) did not spell the disappearance of the human teller; it merely shifted the responsibilities of those employees dealing directly with customers away from handling deposits and withdrawals and toward (say) the marketing of credit cards, consumer loans, and other banking services. The ATM, in turn, represents a highly visible example of what Jonathan Gershuny identifies as the rise of a "self-service" economy, in which tasks formerly performed by paid employees are imposed on consumers: the automated teller replaces the bank employee's labor not with a machine, but with the free labor of its user.[9]

Automation of a particular sector or group of occupations—a large number of clerical positions, for example—will often have paradoxical effects not only on that sector, but on other, seemingly unrelated, segments of the labor market as well. Within the sector directly affected by the introduction of labor-saving devices, as we have seen, the rapidly declining cost of the good or service produced by automated means will often drive up demand for it: such goods are said to be price elastic, with tight correlations between price movements and output. The rising demand for such goods and services will draw in labor, the introduction of labor-saving techniques. This expanding demand for labor will therefore offset some of the labor-shedding effects of the new machinery. Price elasticity has limits: as the cost of electronics like televisions and cellular phones falls year after year, more potential consumers can afford them. But because most individual consumers are unlikely to own and use more than one cellular phone, even massive reductions in prices for these goods will not compel consumers to buy more of them. Food is perhaps the best example of this phenomenon. As food becomes ever cheaper in industrialized societies, owing to extraordinary advances in agricultural techniques (fertilizers, farm equipment, supply-chain management, and so on), the total quantity of food consumed does not grow in step with these advances.

Consumers are more inclined to buy other things, primarily services, including food served in restaurants. Indeed, it is this very dynamic—the rising consumption of services in response to cheaper and cheaper manufactured goods—that explains in no small part the rise of cheap personal services, and the growing number of workers allocated to these types of jobs. Service industries like childcare, education, restaurants, and cleaning are described by economists as income elastic, meaning the demand for them rises in response to rising incomes: the more income households have, the more they will spend on childcare, nannies, gardeners, and maids. This is so even in a world of stagnant incomes: as long as the *share* of income spent on manufactured goods like clothes, electronics, and automobiles declines, a larger part of a household's (and a national economy's) total income can and will be spent on personal services.

"New technology and productivity growth in other areas," Autor notes, "may therefore *indirectly* raise demand for manual task-intensive occupations." As certain goods and services become cheaper through productivity increases in one sector, the demand for labor-intensive services in others will rise.[10] This rising demand for labor will absorb and offset declining demand in the technologically progressive sectors. As I have discussed in detail in a previous chapter, the reallocation of labor to low-productivity service occupations drives down aggregate labor productivity. As more and more labor accumulates in these low-skill, low-productivity areas, the competition for these jobs is fierce and wages are held down in response. The low wages resulting from an oversupply of labor in turn "blocks the mechanization of these branches of production," since rising wages are one of the primary drivers of automation.[11]

Here we hit upon the secret of automation's effects on the broader labor market. Automation impacts specific sectors of the economy, not the economy as a whole; if it drives up labor productivity in one sector, it can hold down productivity in another. There is a fundamental structural unevenness in the distribution of automation's effects: it takes back with one hand what it gives with the other. This explains why the rising labor productivity in one sector results in little to no net gains in productivity across the economy. Despite the predictions, fearful or optimistic, of the pundits of automation, something like "full" automation of the economy—the uniform application of automation across all sectors, with a resulting replacement by machines of all or most of the labor employed—is impossible in a social formation founded on wage-labor. Here the resistance to automation comes less from the nature of the labor process than from the fact that, in a world of abundant cheap labor, there is no compulsion to economize on labor inputs.

The bottom tier of the job market made up in large part of service occupations is resistant to wholesale automation *because* labor-saving innovation is happening elsewhere in the economy: labor-process refinements in other sectors shed workers who, because they must work to live, are shunted into low-wage, low-skill occupations. This surfeit of available labor creates intense competition for otherwise undesirable jobs, holding wages down. There can be an oversupply of labor in this sector, though, because these jobs are deemed to require little to no pre-existing skill, requiring no special training or aptitude to perform the tasks associated with them. In many cases, workers who hold these positions are trained on the job, or at most subject to short introductory training sessions or programs before they begin.

There is a certain irony bound up with defining these jobs as requiring no skills. Though their resistance to automation stems primarily from the cheap labor that accumulates in these sectors, the types of work required in service occupations are also, in material terms, difficult to replicate with machines. Complex mental and intellectual operations that nevertheless obey a set of rules or a formalizable grammar are susceptible to being programmed for and learned by machines, while "simple" tasks like cleaning a room or watching a child require styles of spatial perception and calculation, manual and physical dexterity, not to mention an implicit understanding of norms like what "clean" or "safe" mean in a given situation, that have stymied attempts at mimicry by machines. What is more, because many of these jobs involve direct person-to-person interaction, they require familiarity with intricate sets of linguistic and social conventions through which a given jobholder must interpret needs and desires, often from patients or children who might have difficulty articulating them.

Historically, in the context of the factory and the assembly line, semi- or low-skill labor processes were defined by the degree of routineness or predictability required by the activity: a highly refined detail division of labor isolated specific segments of the process, reducing them to a few easily repeated tasks. Today, the definition is turned on its head: low-skill labor is identified with unpredictable, highly intuitive decisions and activities that are nevertheless deemed "human" or "natural," instinctual or innate, even though they tend to be subtle, learned capacities cultivated within the context of private or family life rather than in school or at work. Indeed, there is a perverse symmetry or mirroring between the two extremes of the increasingly polarized labor market. While mid-level but routine clerical or administrative activities are subject, and according to some studies increasingly vulnerable, to labor-saving innovations, the upper and lower tiers of employment—those deemed high- and low-skill occupations— remain largely impervious to the same encroachments, because in each case the labor process is rooted in implied or intuitive knowledge and decision-making, and often high levels of inter-personal contact. What distinguishes them, in fact, is that in the case of high-skill occupations the person-to-person relations often take the form not of direct interaction with customers or clients, but management of the labor force itself.

When we speak of skill, then, we are by no means referring to some objective measure of difficulty or complexity of the required task. The category of skill is social through and through. A primary feature of this category is the presence or absence of "barriers to entry" for a particular job tier: "highly skilled" occupations are available to a much smaller pool of workers, putting less downward pressure on the compensation—it is not clear we should speak of *wages* in many cases—these jobs are allocated. Eligibility for these positions is primarily determined by education levels, and the compensation levels associated with them are in part determined by the cost of reproducing a similar set of qualifications.

A broadly Marxist perspective is useful here, however fragmented, confusing, or even confused Marx's own remarks on the hierarchy of so-called simple and complex labor might be. Marx's fundamental insight is that the value of labor-power, represented in money terms by the wage, has nothing to do with the value created by labor in production. One of the great errors of both spontaneous and theoretical accounts of the wage is to imagine it is determined by the amount of value contributed by this or that worker in the production process: the higher wages of so-called skilled workers accurately reflect, in this account, the value they contribute in relation to that contributed by lower-paid, less skilled workers. Not so. Instead, the value of labor-power in Marx's formulation refers to the cost of the goods and services necessary to reproduce a given capacity to labor, day-in and day-out and over the course of generations. These costs include seemingly elementary needs (food, shelter, clothing, healthcare) whose definitions shift historically and differ widely among regions at any given historical moment (compare the norms of adequate nutrition, housing, and so on in France and Vietnam). Within a given labor market, however, these core needs and the cost of their reproduction are supplemented by a grid of skill levels that in turn determine the wage hierarchy, that is, how the wage share of social product is distributed among wage-earners. The measure of high- as opposed to middle- or low-skill occupations is determined primarily by the cost of acquiring the specialized knowledge or know-how, counted in money and in time (in marginalist terms, the decision to pursue higher education involves the "opportunity cost" of wages foregone during that period). The cost of reproducing a laboring capacity deemed highly skilled, and requiring high levels of formal education, is the primary factor in the determination of the price of this labor. By the same token, the value of labor-power deemed unskilled is much lower, since the cost of its reproduction is restricted to a minimum set of necessary goods and services.

Those occupations deemed highly skilled command higher wages than other workers not because they contribute more value to the labor process and the final product than other moments of the division of labor, but because the cost of reproducing their specific skill sets is, in monetary terms, higher. As a result, within the dynamics of the labor market, these workers are shielded from competition for these positions from a large part of the existing labor force; their expensive educations function as insuperable barriers to entry for other workers, and offer them rent-like wage premiums.[12]

High-skill occupations in many cases entail managerial tasks or supervisory labor, which separates this activity from wage-labor, properly speaking. The skill and wage levels of these workers cannot be attributed to their "productivity." Far from being more productive than other workers, many well-paid positions in contemporary capitalist economies are decidedly unproductive, in the Marxist sense of not producing any value (or surplus-value) at all: their wages are costs shouldered by capitalist firms as a price of doing business. Doing business, in this case, often means overseeing other workers; the worker is responsible for ensuring that other workers are producing as much value—and surplus-value—as is possible for a given labor process. This specific skill, the supervising of other workers, makes the wage earned by these workers something more than a mere wage. The compensation offered such employees, who act as delegates of owners of capital, can be considered a share of the profits these owners accumulate, disguised as salary or wages.

Finally, it is no accident that occupations classified as requiring few or no skills have traditionally been understood as "women's work," notably the preparation and serving of food and caring for the young, the old, and the sick. No one would deny that, in the latter cases in particular, such activities are skilled, measured in objective terms: they are difficult, and require the mobilization of forms of knowledge as well as physical, emotional, and social capacities that many mid-level skill occupations— clerical work, for example—do not. Yet because these capacities are developed primarily within the family, and are performed and transmitted, without pay, by and among women, the costs of their reproduction are negligible. Historically, these activities were often performed in the home; when women entered the workforce en masse, beginning in the 1970s, they often found themselves performing these same roles outside the home for wages. In addition to the minimal costs required to reproduce this labor, there is a stigma attached to this work that holds down the wages earned by these workers: if this is work done for free in the home, it will be done for minimal wages outside the home. Even when these activities are assumed by men, they *remain women's work*, and are paid accordingly. This implicit gendering of this work, and the way this bias helps hold down the wages these jobs earn, serves to reinforce the more objective constraints exerting downward pressure. In addition to the sheer availability of workers "qualified" to perform these services—since no *skills* are required to perform them, and because skilled workers displaced by rising productivity elsewhere in the economy are shunted into this sector— employers who hire such workers know, because most of their expenses take the form of labor costs, that their own bottom lines are directly affected by rising (or falling) wages. Because these occupations are labor-intensive in the extreme, often employing little to no fixed capital and relatively small quantities of raw materials, the profit share of income for businesses specializing in these services is directly determined by labor's share.

The growing bottom end of the labor market, featuring low-productivity services, is not unique to the u.s. Over roughly the same time period, all sixteen of the European nations considered in a recent study experienced similar patterns of employment polarization, their low-wage service sectors expanding relative to middle-income occupations.[13] A particularly significant case study is Germany. Long hailed as a model of fiscal discipline and economic dynamism, with its modest but steady GDP growth, low unemployment, and enviable trade surpluses, it was in 1999 diagnosed by *The Economist* as "the sick man of Europe."[14] Throughout the 1990s, on the heels of the reunification of West with East Germany, the German economy lagged far behind the rest of Europe on a number of fronts: growth was lower than most of the continent, exports were declining, fiscal deficits exceeded Maastricht limits, and the unemployment rate soared to 10 percent or more, a level more commonly associated with the traditionally sluggish economies of the Mediterranean basin (Spain, Italy, Greece). The imperative to absorb and to some extent dismantle the economy of the old GDR, with its "16 million people, thousands of outdated smokestack factories and a 50-year legacy of central planning," was undoubtedly one source of these ills.[15] The pressure was such that, by the beginning of the new millennium, an ambitious round of reforms was undertaken by Gerhard Schroeder, who came to power through his Social Democratic Party's alliance with the German Greens. The specifics of the program were developed by and named after Peter Hartz, Volkswagen's head of human resources; the objective was to put Germans "back to work" while also restoring growth, fiscal discipline, and German competitiveness on the global scene. The plan, officially called Agenda 2010, took an axe to long-standing labor market protections and benefits provisions while also imposing wage restraints, all with the blessing and muscle of the typically obedient German unions.

The upshot of the reforms was to force unemployed workers to take any job that became available to them through newly formed job centers, no matter the pay, conditions, or how poorly their own skills matched the job listing. One observer characterized the reforms in these terms: "Hartz IV [the fourth phase of the reforms] is essentially a compulsory precarious-employment service," one that created a new and vast pool of working poor in one of the world's richest nations.[16] Though official unemployment figures have fallen dramatically since these new measures were implemented, with more and more Germans categorized as "having jobs," the number of hours worked has risen much more modestly, barely above the numbers registered in the mid-1990s. This is due to the fact that many of these jobs are part-time, temporary, or otherwise do not meet the standards of full employment set after the Second World War. The jobs "miracle," often touted both by German officials and by European politicians—especially the French, on the right and the left—envious of the ease with which these reforms were rolled out, has a hint of the Potemkin village about it. The result has been less the mobilization of the full might of the German labor market than the reclassification of the unemployed as nominal job holders, at the cost of a significant increase in workers deemed "at risk of poverty." Germany now has one of the largest low-wage sectors in Europe, with one in five workers said to be "low-paid," that is, earning less than two-thirds of the median wage.[17]

While some observers argue that these labor market reforms were largely responsible for Germany's current position within the global economy—they are, *The Economist* declares, "one of the main foundations of Germany's current economic boom [by making] labour newly competitive and have kept productivity high"[18]—others attribute this new "competitiveness" to an early initiative taken by "unions and work councils to hold down wage growth," and in so doing

> [help] German businesses adapt to a higher level of international competition. In the light of high unemployment, both [unions and businesses] agreed to preserve jobs rather than increase wages. The Hartz reforms gave the screw another turn at the bottom of the wage distribution, but most of the wage restraint had happened beforehand.[19]

Indeed, the German Trade Union Federation (DGB), dominated by unions in established heavy industries like metallurgy and chemicals, refused to militate against the SDP's broad make-work program, despite the predictable effects it would have on the German labor markets and working class. Their mandate, they claimed, was the defense of their own members "through sectoral agreement," little more. On the political level, the impositions of these reforms led not only to the defection of a significant fraction of the SDP's traditional working-class base, but to the splitting off of the left wing of the party and the formation of *Die Linke*, the sole parliamentary party opposed to the gutting of labor market protections. This splintering of the broad German left—now comprised of the Social Democrats, the Greens, and *Die Linke*—in turn opened the path to power for Angela Merkel's center-right Christian Democratic Party. She has held the post of chancellor of Germany since 2005, and will remain in place until 2021.

seven

An Absolute Law

There is a passage that crops up in the midst of Marx's *Capital* that captures one of the key paradoxes of what he calls the specifically capitalist application of machinery. At first glance, the scenario Marx draws out seems far removed from our own time in its details. But closer inspection reveals a surprising continuity with the condition of many wage-laborers today, both in the rich nations of Europe and North America, and *a fortiori* for workers elsewhere across the globe. The paradox is this: in many situations when available labor-saving machinery can or should be used, it isn't. In a non-capitalist society, one can imagine labor-saving machinery would be used first and foremost to perform the most onerous and least desirable tasks considered socially necessary. These are jobs that in many cases put a special physical, mental, or emotional strain on workers; often, they are jobs that compromise the health of those compelled to perform them, leading over time to physical and emotional harm, eventually an inability to work at all. In advanced capitalist economies, these workers, now deprived of the ability to work, often find themselves reclassified as "disabled." Others will die before their time. But in the case of many such workers, in particular women, being unemployed and disabled does not mean a release from the burden of work. At home, there are often men, perhaps also disabled or out of work, to be looked after, along with children (including adult children) who require attention. Sometimes parents or older relatives are present, requiring care. The invisible labor in the home must be done even if, in the eyes of the state, these workers are deemed unable to work. It is performed without compensation and almost always alone and in private, without the cooperation of others, and with minimal technological mediation (at best, a washing machine for the clothes, television for the children).

These sorts of activities, however necessary they may be for the reproduction of capitalist class relations, are always the last to be rationalized, that is, made more efficient, and less onerous, by means of labor-saving innovations. I have already discussed in detail the reasons for this. In some cases, the labor process itself is hard to reproduce mechanically. If you think robots have a hard time driving cars, imagine the calamities simple tasks like folding clothes or giving baths to the elderly would entail. But just as often, the pressure to automate activities is obviated by the sheer availability of human labor-power, which cheapens the cost of labor and therefore discourages business owners from investing capital in expensive machinery that often becomes obsolete well before it fully depreciates. An abundance of labor means a dearth of machines.

When Marx sketches out the many "contradictions and antagonisms inseparable from the capitalist application of machinery," he is particularly sensitive to the claims made by business owners and their advocates, economists, regarding the blessings machines hold in store *for workers*, who in the first decades of the workers' movement saw them as a threat to their livelihood. Citing John Stuart Mill, he begins his chapter on machinery by calling into question whether "all the mechanical inventions yet made have lightened the day's toil of any human being."[1] Marx offers a litany of paradoxes generated by the contradictions that arise from innovation, which renders human labor more productive in material terms (things or services produced per unit of labor) and less productive in money terms (since less value-producing labor-power is consumed in the labor process). One of the most poignant images he elaborates comes early on in the chapter, when he observes that in England, the home of the industrial revolution, wage-laborers are forced to perform particularly dreadful labors that are elsewhere carried out either by machines, or by beasts of burden. "In England," he writes, women

> are still occasionally used instead of horses for hauling barges, because the labour required to produce horses and machines is an accurately known quantity, while that required to maintain the women of the surplus population is beneath all calculation. Hence we nowhere find a more shameless squandering of human labour-power for despicable purposes than in England, the land of machinery.[2]

Not only is machinery abundant and cheaply available in England, where much of it is invented and produced, it is also shipped across the seas to North America and Europe, where it performs tasks that the "women of the surplus population" perform in England. It is more rational for a business owner to pay unemployed women to haul barges than to hire horses or employ machines, since capitalists who compete with one another in a given sector must choose the cheapest combination of inputs (labor, raw materials, machinery, rents, and so on) possible relative to a given quantity of work performed. To do otherwise is to risk losing business to competitors and, eventually, face bankruptcy. The paradox outlined in this passage, however, is not simply that a surplus of available labor drives down wages, which in turn deters business owners from replacing certain types of laboring activities with machines. The excess of labor that prevents the mechanization or automation of one particular sector is itself the result of an "excess" of automation in another sector.

In highly industrialized economies, Marx observes, the use of efficient, labor-saving devices in one industry, for example in the textile factories, will often temporarily create such a redundancy of labor in that industry that a large number of workers will be displaced into other sectors of the economy, desperate for work. Because they need money to survive, they will perform whatever odd jobs present themselves, and do so for wages that are a fraction of what they were formerly paid in their previous job. Under these circumstances, wages will be pushed downward by the supply of labor, so much so that the wages received will fall below the established value of labor-power. When the price of labor-power dips below its value, the cost of labor is so low that it actively "*prevents* the use of machinery in [these] other branches and, from the standpoint of the capitalist, makes the use of machinery superfluous, and *often impossible*, because his profit comes from a reduction in the labor paid for, not in the labor employed."[3] If what determines whether a capitalist employs machinery is whether the cost of the labor objectified in the machine is lower than the cost of the labor it displaces, then a precipitous drop in wages can effectively prevent a business owner from employing machinery, even should he or she want to do so. Yet this paradoxical condition, in which machines are left to idle, or shipped overseas where wages are higher, *is itself an effect of the capitalist application of machines*: a sudden surge in technological innovation in one sector will produce, ineluctably and in an uneven pattern, technological stagnation in another.

Marx's chapter on "machinery and large-scale industry" is by far the longest chapter of *Capital*, and it is also the chapter richest in empirical data about contemporary British industry, much of it gathered from the reports of factory inspectors commissioned by parliament to examine the living and employment conditions of the English working class. The period in which Marx was writing was one marked by the rapid mechanization of certain industries. The textile industry was especially affected by this historical process, bringing together a stream of innovations in technology and refinements of the labor process, reflecting advances in the natural sciences and engineering, and an enormous boom in raw materials, especially cotton, shipped from the slave plantations of the u.s. South to the docks of Liverpool, on their way to Manchester and the industrial heartlands. Marx notes throughout this chapter not only the increasing number of workers absorbed into the fast-growing textile industries but the equally prodigious growth of ancillary industries, which reflected the dynamism of England's manufacturing core. The explosion in labor productivity in the textile factories abetted a boom not only in raw materials produced overseas by slave labor, but in local industries as well: in machine production, in the extraction of coal, and in the expansion of the material infrastructure required to distribute these cheap commodities pumped out by the northern English factories. Marx underlines, for example, that whole new industries arose on the heels of the expanding textile industry, and with them new forms of work and new figures of the worker ("along with the machine, a new type of worker springs to life: the machine-maker"). The production of machinery would be supplemented by "entirely new branches of production, creating new fields of labor," in particular the construction of vast facilities capable of shuttling commodities across continents and seas ("canals, docks, tunnels, bridges, and so on"), not to mention new forms of media and communications, such as the telegraph, allowing industrialists and merchants to communicate in real time with suppliers and eventually consumers half a world away.

But in witnessing this prodigious expansion of capitalist economy, which by the time *Capital* was written was global in scale, Marx was particularly sensitive to what he saw as the limits to the expansion of English and, eventually, global industry, despite the fact that the number of workers absorbed into the industrial core (manufacturing, mining, construction) would continue to expand while producing ever more output for almost a full century more. What was especially prescient about Marx's analysis of the arc of capitalist development is the way he measured the historically unprecedented economic growth he observed against what he called *an absolute law*. This law is expressed with the utmost simplicity, even though its ramifications would preoccupy Marx for the rest of his analysis of capitalism. Simply put, it states that "if the total quantity of the article produced by machinery is equal to the quantity of the article previously produced by a handicraft or a manufacture, then total labor expended is diminished."[4] Put this way, the law is almost tautological: provided the same amount of physical output is produced, machinery reduces the quantity of labor needed to produce that output. But Marx's argument is primarily about the effect automating one industry has on job growth in others. Generally speaking, he writes, though the mechanization of one industry "throws men out of work in those industries in which it is introduced," it often in turn "bring[s] about an increase in other employment in other industries." I have already detailed in what sense this is true: the automation of one industry means higher demand for labor in other industries like the production of machines, the cultivation, extraction, or processing of raw materials, and the building of infrastructure like ports and highways. The extent to which these ancillary sectors will expand depends on their degree of capital intensity. The surge in demand for coal (today, we might substitute lithium for electric batteries) to power factories increased the demand for coal miners; yet as coal mines became increasingly mechanized, the demand for miners diminished. But the absolute law of capitalist development posits a clear limit to the growth in demand for labor: it will grow only to the extent that total output of industry ("the total quantity of the article produced" in all industries) does, and necessarily at a slower rate. This applies to individual sectors as much as to the economy as a whole. The growing superfluity of labor in the economy is not simply a pattern that follows the rise and fall of the business cycle; it is a secular and irrevocable trend that Marx elsewhere called the growing immiseration of the proletariat.

Where will these increasingly superfluous workers go, if they are not absorbed into ancillary industries like mining, construction or shipping, transport, and communications? Marx has already given us one image of the fate of such workers: the women of the surplus population, performing the work of horses. But he also points in another direction: an ever-growing "servant class." In the period in which Marx was writing, he noted with irony and rage that the number of English workers employed as servants ("men-servants, women-servants, lackeys, etc.") in the houses of the middle and upper classes exceeded the number of workers employed in the textile industries and mining (both coal and metal extraction), combined. Here, then, is perhaps the greatest contradiction or paradox of the automated factory, as Marx envisioned it:

> the extraordinary increase in the productivity of large-scale industry, accompanied as it is by a more intensive and a more extensive exploitation of labor-power in all other spheres of production, permits a larger and larger part of the working class to be employed unproductively. Hence it is possible to reproduce the ancient domestic slaves, on a constantly expanding scale, under the name of a servant class.[5]

What Marx proposed in his formulation of an absolute law of capitalist development appears to fly in the face of many of the projections developed by socialists and labor-movement militants over the past two centuries. In those accounts, Marx's contention that more and more of the working-age population of industrializing countries would become dependent on wage-labor for its own reproduction is confused with the idea that wage-earning activities will take the form of high-productivity, semi-skilled work in technologically progressive sectors ("modern industry") like manufacturing and mining. Such prognostications seemed, for a full century, to be on the mark, as capital-intensive goods-producing sectors of the economy drew in larger and larger numbers of workers; the manufacturing share of employment expanded in the u.s. and the uk for decades after Marx proposed his absolute law, well into the middle of the twentieth century. It peaked around 1955, that is, at precisely the moment when "automation" began to be implemented on a vast scale in the most productive industries of the global capitalist economy, such as automobiles, steel, mining, and petrochemicals.

A threshold was reached. The very "productiveness of modern industry" meant that fewer and fewer workers, relative to the total working population, were needed to carry out these activities. The productivity gains that meant larger output could be generated with fewer and fewer workers directly involved in its production required more and more workers to be employed in manufacturing-adjacent industries, many of them categorized by Marx as "circulation labor," like transportation and warehousing, retail and sales, accounting and law, communications and infrastructure, and, in the twentieth century, advertising and marketing. But these fast-expanding parallel sectors could not grow rapidly enough to absorb all of the labor shed by productivity gains in the most dynamic sectors. Because these activities will not increase at a rate rapid enough to soak up labor market excess—and many of these activities will be subject to technological "progress" in their turn—a sizable fraction of the wage-earning class will find themselves performing domestic duties for the urban upper and middle classes. Here is a core contradiction of the capitalist use of machinery: the very productivity of capitalist industry consigns a larger and larger portion of humanity to low-productivity, and often unproductive in Marx's sense of the term, laboring activities.

Many observers, primarily on the left, would argue that the picture I have drawn in these pages—a scenario that in my view

confirms Marx's "absolute law" of capital development—is
misleading at best, dispiriting at worst. In a 2016 essay sizing
up the prospects for the U.S. working class, for example, Kim
Moody sketched a portrait of the U.S. economy that appears
to invert, point-by-point, the features I have tried to outline.
Though he conceded the self-evident fact of a considerable
reallocation of labor away from core industries, he suggested
that this migration of workers has had little effect on the key
indicators I have examined. The most salient feature of the U.S.
economy since 1980, he argued, is the "large productivity gains"
achieved by U.S. business, by means of "growing investment and
work intensification."[6] Indeed, contrary to data I have marshalled
in previous chapters regarding the rate of business investment,
Moody claims, against the evidence,[7] that non-residential fixed
investment as a share of GDP has soared since 1980, stabilizing
at a rate higher than in the postwar boom, and has continued
to do so *in the midst of a sustained near-depression*. This surge in
investment in fixed capital, combined with a wave of mergers
and acquisitions beginning in the 1980s, has resulted not only
in impressive gains in labor productivity but in workplace
conditions resembling those that prevailed in earlier phases of
capitalist development: "more and more workers are employed
in workplaces that are both more capital intensive and employ
more workers on average."

Moody is particularly interested in the growth of the so-called
logistics sector, and the way that the reallocation of labor in the
U.S. economy toward circulation activities requires the concentration of workers in a few dense "nodes" or clusters, within which
working conditions resemble those of the old manufacturing
centers of the 1930s–60s: large numbers of workers handling,
valorizing, and potentially arresting, through workplace actions,
enormous quantities of capital. But it is not only these transportation nodes—which in fact employ a tiny portion of the workforce,
and which are expanding at a much slower rate than low-wage

service work—that in Moody's estimation are re-creating conditions reminiscent of the heyday of the u.s. labor movement. Similar trajectories, he holds, can be observed in other sectors, including those traditionally considered "service" occupations. Moody singles out the healthcare sector in particular in his depiction of the trend toward concentrations of capital in larger firms and workplaces combined with rising capital intensity, but nowhere does he make mention of the Bureau of Labor Statistics' contention that job growth in this sector will most likely consist in adding more and more units of low-wage, low-skill labor. Whether he is considering transportation nodes, hospitals and healthcare centers, "Big Box retailers . . . hotels and call centers," Moody sees not dispersed, labor-intensive, low-productivity occupations, but instead "the 'factories' of today," from which a new epoch of "working class organization and action," on a par with the industrial unionism of the 1930s, might once again arise.

Throughout this book, I have marshalled evidence contrary to such a vision. The advanced industrial economies of the world face significant, often mutually reinforcing, headwinds: low productivity growth, declining rates of business investment, stagnant wages, a larger and larger "overhang" of workers who produce no value, faltering profit rates, and so on. All of these conditions represent barriers to what Moody calls "working class organization and action," at least in the form these assumed in the middle of the twentieth century. What must be undertaken today is a sober assessment of these conditions and their effect on the capacity of workers to organize themselves across a complex, fragmented economy, marked by increasing divergence among them, in terms of wage levels, notions of skill, labor processes, and so on.

A widely cited paper from the late 1990s on the causes of deindustrialization, written under the auspices of the International Monetary Fund, sizes up in its conclusion the potential effects of the growing concentration of employment in the slow-growth, technologically stagnant service sector of the economy. The co-authors, Robert Rowthorn and Ramana Ramaswamy, emphasize how the fragmentation of this sector, riven by cleavages in skills and wage levels, combined with the material disparity of the concrete labor processes lumped together under this label, will undoubtedly pose insurmountable obstacles to rebuilding powerful trade unions like the UAW of the late 1930s sit-down strikes. "Trade unions," they warn, "have traditionally derived their strength from industry, where the modes of production and the standardized nature of the work have made it easier to organize workers."[8] The historical workers' movement and the industrial unions of the mid-twentieth century endeavored, through the institution of collective-bargaining agreements, to reduce wage differentials across industries. This objective was formulated not simply on the basis of infra-class solidarity among workers, but on the tendency, driven by competitive pressures among firms, for technological innovations to spread across lines of production and eventually sectors. As firms across the economy adopt similar techniques, the different working conditions of various class segments are smoothed out and over. The rising ratio of machinery and raw materials to labor employed assures a tendential material density of the class. Comparable skill levels, wages, and working conditions prevail in massive plants bringing together thousands of workers at each individual site. The workers' movement itself was at once the product and the reflection of this convergent material unity of the capitalist mode of production: if worker struggles of the nineteenth century (such as the conflicts over the length of the working day) in part spurred the development of the forces of production, the generalization of this development across lines of production in the early twentieth century shaped the class into a compact and often militant mass. This is what James Boggs, a militant auto worker writing in the early 1960s, had in mind when, echoing Marx, he spoke of the "embryo of a socialist society" gestating within this one, "united, disciplined and organized by capitalist production itself."[9]

In her magisterial history of the workers' movement, *Forces of Labor*, Beverly Silver underlines the way the objective splintering of the service sector outlined by Rowthorn and Ramaswamy is reflected in the isolation of these workers from one another, and their distance from the strategic leverage points enjoyed by workers in fields as different as manufacturing and education. Those who work in the automotive industry are imbricated in a tightly articulated detail division of labor, so that a work stoppage at one point in the production sequence can bring the entire process to a halt. Teachers, on the other hand, operate with relative autonomy in their classrooms, less affected by a ramified technical division of labor. At the same time, a large-scale strike by educators might reveal their crucial place in the social division of labor, causing widespread disruption at least at the local level, as parents scramble to find someone to care for their children. Workers in the oil sector, however tiny it may be, are able to disrupt the entire functioning of the capitalist economy on at least the national level, as recent struggles in France (in 2010 and 2016) have shown. Workers who find themselves stranded in low-wage service occupations in retail or hospitality (together, one-fifth of the workforce) have no such leverage: their workplaces are often dispersed and small in comparison with the great industrial concentrations of the past, and they have little fixed capital to idle. Silver can point to important if modest recent victories by workers in these fields, but avers that such successes have come despite the distance of these workplaces—in the case of retail, restaurants, and similar types of work—from the levers of production and social reproduction. They have instead had to "follow a community-based organizing model rather than a model that relies on the positional power of workers at the point of production."[10] It is, however, these pre-existing community ties—neighborhoods, languages, religion—that the ever-expanding ambit of the personal services sector threatens. If these were the foundations of the old workers' movement, whose forms of mutuality and self-aid often relied on affinities derived from ethnic, cultural, and geographical proximity, they are today everywhere in tatters, as the social fabric is chewed through by the corrosive effects of money and markets, and communities dissipate into warring, atomized dysfunction.

By far the most militant section of the u.s. labor force in the recent past has been not workers in large industrial firms with high capital-to-labor ratios but public-sector workers in the "education industry." The past few years have witnessed large-scale, even state-wide, strikes by teachers, especially in politically conservative American states, with deep support from the public, who are often parents directly affected by such work stoppages. (The 2019 strike by Los Angeles Unified School District employees shares many of the features of the strikes in rural, Republican states.) These strikes in most cases won modest gains for teachers, both in terms of direct and indirect wages—West Virginia teachers first organized, defensively, against dramatic increases in insurance premiums—and with regard to deteriorating working conditions, including rising class sizes, the lack of nurses in schools, and encroachment on public education from privately run "charter schools." In most cases, the demands that triggered the strikes were formulated not by the leadership of the public sector unions, in the framework of traditional collective bargaining agreements, but by rank-and-file pressure, through the use of social media and novel tactics developed *in situ*. Above all, these strikes seemed to have a political content: they represented a spirited defense of the public sector as a cost necessary for the reproduction of society. Though teachers are subject to few of the constraints and pressures of private-sector employees in industries where technological change—and the broader search for efficiencies—drives individual employers in fierce competition with other firms for market share, they play a considerable part in the production of a competent workforce able to supply the job market with fresh, semi-skilled and cheap labor-power. In addition to this longer-term objective, forming workers able to read, write, and learn new skills, teachers and educational personnel perform a perhaps even more important role in the day-to-day functioning of society: they watch over, care for, and manage tens of millions of children so that their parents, in particular women, can earn money through wage-labor elsewhere in the social division of labor.

We can underline here the stark contrast between the material situation of workers in the education industry, in particular teachers, and the private-sector workers in heavily capitalized industries whom Moody anticipates will be most agitated in the years to come. Workers in education are subject to few of the factors he cites as conditions for an epoch of renewed labor militancy. The "changes in the labor process" he claims are "embracing" more and more of the working class—technological change, concentration of industries, rising capital-to-labor ratios, just-in-time supply chains—do not affect this particular industry even indirectly, for the most part. The actual labor process required in the delivery of education services has changed very little over decades, or even longer, whatever enthusiasm administrators might have for introducing new technologies in the classroom. Indeed, despite the ever-expanding administrative stratum of the industry, and the corresponding oversight functions it carries out, classroom activities are marked by a high degree of autonomy relative to other kinds of work. Though some activities associated with teaching have been reassigned to teacher's assistants, one of the fastest growing jobs in the post-crisis economy, the technical division of labor at the classroom level is almost non-existent, especially relative to the massive industrial concerns of the 1930s Moody sees as models for the "factories of today." Educators remain relatively immune to the pressures of so-called automation. "Productivity" gains can be wrung from teachers for the most part only by expanding classroom size, decreasing teacher-to-student ratios, and having some of their traditional functions carried out by less skilled assistants. It is against these cost-cutting measures, long the only recourse of administrators, that teachers have mobilized. And just as teachers are invulnerable to most forms of techno-logical substitution, they are also not subject to offshoring or replacement by cheaper labor elsewhere. In contrast with those sectors of the private economy focused on producing tradable goods and services, the education industry cannot exploit wage differentials across geographical distances; by the same token, the services it provides cannot be concentrated in just a few regional "clusters," as with the logistics industry. In *Forces of Labor*, written well before the current upsurge, Beverly Silver suggests that "the imperviousness of the education industry to spatial and technological fixes (in particular, geographical relocation and automation) may be at the root of a great deal of teacher bargaining power."[11]

In order to understand why the movement of teachers has been as powerful as it has been, we should employ a crucial distinction between two forms of the division of labor. Specializ-ation is a feature of modern, industrial societies: individual units of production tend to focus on making a single product or related group of products (Nike, for example, does not make frozen yogurt), while workers are generally given skill-specific tasks within these units. The segmentation of production tasks within a given unit of production is generally referred to as the detail, or technical, division of labor; the specialization of production, with individual firms focused on a narrow range of products, across the economy as a whole is called the social division of labor.

In conceptual terms, we can say that the detail division of labor within a given unit of production (a single company, for example) requires both the segmentation of the labor process into discrete tasks, and the coordination of these separated activities by managers who plan and oversee this unified process. In the case of the social division of labor, the distribution and coordination of specialized activities is organized not through deliberate planning but by means of the market. Within a given company, individual segments of the labor process are not coordinated through exchange; one workshop in a car factory does not purchase inputs from another workshop within the same factory. In advanced economies, however, particularly in a context of globalized trade relations and wage differentials across geographical distances, even the production of relatively simple products can incorporate components from a wide variety of producers often separated by both large distances and national borders. A production process that might, decades ago, have been largely done in-house, today is turned outward, mobilizing intricate supply chains punctuated by acts of buying and selling, with the final product assembled from any number of produced inputs. In such a scenario, the distinction between the detail and social divisions of labor becomes tenuous, entwining internal planning and exchange between distinct producers. By the same token, in an economy in which the principles of planning predominate, an altogether different relation between these two forms prevails: rather than market relations intervening within the production of a single commodity, the planning process extends beyond the unit of production to society as a whole.

Moody's mapping of the "new terrain" of class struggle in an era of globalized production emphasizes the way transnational supply chains create an extended technical division of labor, in which workers involved in the transportation, handling, and storing of products performed by the so-called "logistics" industry can be said to "perform final steps in actual production," and to be "engaged in goods production despite being classified as something else by the Bureau of Labor Statistics." The same cannot be said, however, for the material situation in which workers in the education industry find themselves. As I have spelled out already, the efficiencies typical of the technical division of labor are almost entirely absent in the classroom, or in the school system as a whole. A labor stoppage in one workshop at a large factory can bring the entire production process to a halt; a labor stoppage in one classroom in one school will have little effect on the activities of other classrooms, nor will a labor stoppage at one school affect the rest of the school district. But should the teachers and educational laborers of an entire school district go on strike, or otherwise interrupt their labor, the effect will be massive and radiate through the entire economy, as workers in other sectors scramble to find daycare for their children. The power of these workers is attributable not to their place in a technical division of labor but to their place within the social division of labor, since the withdrawal of their labor compels the interruption of work across a given locale. This material leverage, combined with the fact that educational services are only with difficulty replaced by "automation" or threats of relocation, gives these workers a power almost unequaled elsewhere in the economy.

What about the rest of the service sector, given that the workers in the largely public education sector, though in a highly strategic position within the social division of labor, still make up a small fraction of the total workforce? What of those workers who find themselves condemned to the circumstances of isolation and atomization characteristic of the servant economy? The conditions these workers share with teachers is that their jobs remain largely invulnerable to both automation and offshoring. In the first case this is because the tasks performed do not admit replacement by even the most advanced technological innovations; in the second, because these are in-person services performed on site, and so cannot be performed remotely. In contrast with Moody's image of workers concentrated in larger and larger workplaces, in conditions approximating the factories of the great industrial epoch, the growing personal services sector is by its very nature fragmented into small workplaces, and their in-person nature requires these workplaces to be spatially dispersed, rather than being concentrated in a few huge hubs, clusters, or facilities. Here the contrast with teachers is especially important, since those who deliver education services, though their particular place of work might employ a small number of people, invariably work for a single employer encompassing a unified district or territory. These conditions, though hardly factory-like, nevertheless offer workers in this industry opportunities for action not found elsewhere in the workforce. Indeed, in this specific sense, the workplace conditions encountered by teachers do resemble those of the large factories of the 1930s, in which tens of thousands of workers could conduct large-scale and sometimes economically crippling actions against their employers. But the parallel stops there. Workers in techno-logically progressive industries have power through their place in a technical division of labor; teachers, owing to their position within the social division of labor. In the case of workers consigned to jobs in retail, restaurants, and nursing homes, none of these conditions favoring a "coming upsurge" prevail.

France in early 2020 was the site of an enormous and powerful mobilization of workers revolting against changes, proposed by the Macron administration, to the system of retirement benefits. This mobilization not only brought about large and frequent union-led demonstrations, but involved a particularly effective transport strike, in which unionized workers employed by national and regional rail services immobilized entire cities and regions for weeks on end, preventing many workers from using public services to get to and from work. Like the case of the teachers discussed above, here is an instance of a workplace action that, because of the sensitive and strategic place occupied by these public services personnel in the social division of labor, has the potential to quickly set off a widespread, if not total, immobilization of economic activity.

Yet these demonstrations must be seen in relation to another, apparently unrelated, form of class struggle that recently emerged in France. This time, the protagonists were primarily workers living outside of dense urban areas, in regions where there is a relative absence of public services, or where those services have recently been cut back dramatically. The revolt of the *gilets jaunes*, so named because of the yellow safety vests those who took part in these struggles wore as a sign of solidarity, was triggered by a proposed tax on diesel fuel that would inordinately affect those workers, many of whom participate in the low-wage "servant" sector, who must drive to and from work owing to the dearth or withdrawal of state-provided transportation networks. What is specific and new about these struggles is that those who undertook them, unlike the striking rail workers, are not unionized and are unable to undertake workplace actions that would contribute to a broader slowing or shutting down of economic activity. Even if they could, the types of work they do are for the most part not located at key points in the social division of labor, as is the case for transport workers or teachers. It is true that many of those who took part were truck drivers, whose labor is embedded in the extended detail division of labor articulated by the just-in-time production model and its logistics infrastructure. But most of the workers involved find they are "excluded" from the economy in more than one sense: they are paid low wages, forced out of cities, denied public services, are not unionized, and do not perform activities that are located at strategic points in the economy. It is for this reason that their struggle was restricted primarily to Saturdays, when workers have the day off, and that it had little direct effect on workplaces. As a movement, however, it was especially significant insofar as it mobilized workers who are not represented by the traditional institutions of the labor movement. Most had never been to a demonstration before deciding to participate in the movement. The contrast between the struggle undertaken by French public service workers and those who are most affected by the absence of transportation services in the French hinterlands is a telling one, reflecting in the arena of class struggle a deep polarization internal to contemporary capitalist labor markets.

In the early 1960s, Boggs foresaw a day when a large number of those expelled from the factories of northern industry would have "nowhere to go": these were the "surplus people," "the expendables of automation." Today the children and grand-children of these surplus people remain trapped in collapsing cities, far-flung suburbs, and rural ruins. They scrape by on part-time precarious work and tenuous lines of extortionate credit, commuting to and from work an hour each way, surveilled by heavily armed cops as they make their way home from bus stops. Some run rackets and hustles, while others sink into depression or drugs. Prison is always near.

Boggs foresaw a world of outsiders on the margins of the wage relation, whose every move was hounded by money. To those who imagined rebuilding the AFL-CIO of two decades prior, he could only say, dream on. The union was lost, he wrote with *sangfroid*, the moment the bosses brought in the comput-er-controlled machines. The cause of unionism was lost before that: never setting out to attack the bases of capitalist society, it became part of it. "Historically, workers move ahead," Boggs wrote, in imaginary retort to those who want to reactivate older figures of organization. "*That is, they bypass existing organizations and form new ones uncorrupted by past habits and customs.*" Boggs was careful not to venture details about what shapes these organs might take; he did not promise they would reconcile the class fractions churned out by changes in the composition of capital. American workers (a term ample enough to envelop his "surplus people") would, should they take command again over their own lives, have to launch a "revolt powerful enough to smash the union, the company, and the state." But Boggs's accent was less on negation than discovery. Surrounded by "labor leaders and well-meaning liberals" proposing gimmick upon gimmick in hopes of saving the reigning social order, Boggs wagered on these "outsiders," who will have to compose, and soon, a "new way to live." What he said then is just as true now: *"The means to live without having to work are all around them, before their very eyes. The only question, the trick, is how to take them."*[12]

References

Automation 2.0

1 James Boggs, *The American Revolution: Pages from a Negro Worker's Notebook* (New York, 1963), p. 36.
2 John Lewis, "Bitesize: The Past Decade's Productivity Growth in Historical Context," Bank Underground, April 25, 2018, https://bankunderground.co.uk.
3 Robert Solow, "We'd Better Watch Out," *New York Times Book Review*, July 12, 1987, p. 36.
4 Mark Muro, Robert Maxim and Jacob Whiton, The Brookings Institute, "The robots are ready as the COVID-19 recession spreads," March 24, 2020, available at www.brookings.edu.
5 Nitasha Tiku, "Desperate Workers Rush to Delivery App Jobs to find Low Pay and Punishing Rules," *Washington Post*, May 23, 2020, www.washingtonpost.com.

1 A Little History of Automation

1 Erik Loomis, "The Case for a Federal Jobs Guarantee," *New York Times*, April 25, 2018, www.nytimes.com.
2 Peter Frase, *Four Futures: Life after Capitalism* (New York, 2016), p. 9.
3 Carl Benedikt Frey and Michael Osborne, "The Future of Employment: How Susceptible Are Jobs to Computerisation?," Oxford Martin School, September 2013. Frey has recently published a follow-up book, *The Technology Trap: Capital, Labor, and Power in the Age of Automation* (Princeton, NJ, 2019).
4 Stuart W. Elliott, "Anticipating a Luddite Revival," *Issues in Science and Technology*, xxx/3 (Spring 2014), pp. 27–36.
5 Andrew Ure, *The Philosophy of Manufactures; or, An Exposition of the Scientific, Moral, and Commercial Economy of the Factory System of Great Britain* (London, 1835), p. 9.
6 Among Ure's litany of automatic devices, one particularly important self-acting machine is absent: the mechanical clock. The Greek world knew an earlier variant of this mechanism, the *clepsydra* or water

clock, which functioned through the use of constant flows of
water pressure (most Greek automata used either water or air
power). Such clocks measure the passing of time using constant,
invariable units of time. But this abstract time had little effect on
the organization of social life, particularly the "productive" activities
taking place either in the countryside or the cities. These were still
largely regulated by natural cycles and sequences, and the notion
of labor productivity—the measurement of output per given,
constant unit of time—was unknown. On the historical production
of "abstract time" and the invention of the mechanical clock, see
Moishe Postone, *Time, Labor and Social Domination* (Cambridge,
1993), pp. 200ff., and Jacques Le Goff, *Time, Work and Culture in
the Middle Ages*, trans. Arthur Goldhammer (Chicago, IL, 1982).
7   See Book 1, section IV of Aristotle's *Politics*.
8   Rabelais' *Gargantua* was first published in 1532.
9   Amazon named its online platform for a "global, on-demand, 24×7
    workforce" to perform "microtasks" Mechanical Turk, presumably
    because these human workers carry out repetitive tasks machines
    should, but cannot yet, perform. Cf. Ure, *The Philosophy of
    Manufactures*, p. 11. Edgar Allan Poe's famous essay on the device,
    "Maelzel's Chess Player," was published in 1836. In his "Theses
    on the Philosophy of History," Walter Benjamin invoked the
    image of Maelzel's chess player, naming the automaton "historical
    materialism," the hidden chess master, "theology." See "Theses on
    the Philosophy of History," *Selected Writings*, vol. IV, p. 389.
10 Ure, *The Philosophy of Manufactures*, p. 18.
11 Quoted in David Noble, *Forces of Production: A Social History of
    Automation* (Piscataway, NJ, 2011), p. 68. See especially its fourth
    chapter, "Toward the Automatic Factory."
12 Quoted in Frederick Pollock, *Automation: A Study of Its Economic
    and Social Consequences*, trans. W. O. Henderson and W. H. Chaloner
    (New York, 1956), p. 16n.1.
13 Ure, *The Philosophy of Manufactures*, p. 301.
14 Pollock, *Automation*, p. 108.
15 Karl Marx, *Grundrisse: Foundations of the Critique of Political Economy*,
    trans. Martin Nicolaus (Harmondsworth, 1973), p. 705.
16 Thomas O. Boucher, *Computer Automation in Manufacturing:
    An Introduction* (London, 1996), p. 6.
17 Pollock, *Automation*, pp. 82, 82n.1.
18 Ibid., p. 248.
19 James Boggs, *The American Revolution: Pages from a Negro Worker's
    Notebook* (New York, 1963), p. 36.
20 "All Employees: Manufacturing/All Employees: Total Nonfarm
    Payrolls," Federal Reserve Bank of St. Louis, March 2, 2020;
    https://fred.stlouisfed.org.

SMART MACHINES AND SERVICE WORK

21 Bureau of Labor Statistics, "Women in the Labor Force, 1970–2009," *Economics Daily*, January 5, 2001; www.bls.gov.

22 As has the total labor force participation rate since 2000, when it peaked.

23 Cited in Jeremy Rifkin, *The End of Work: The Decline of the Global Labor Force and the Dawn of the Post-market Era* (New York, 1995), p. 141.

24 Rifkin, *The End of Work*, p. 291.

25 Matthew C. Klein, "The Great American Make-work Programme," *Financial Times* Alphaville blog, September 8, 2016; https://ftalphaville.ft.com.

2 The Robot and the Zombie

1 Jean Baudrillard, *The System of Objects*, trans. James Benedict (London, 1996), pp. 124–5.

2 Erik Brynjolfsson and Andrew McAfee,*The Second Machine Age: Work, Progress, and Prosperity in a Time of Brilliant Technologies* (New York and London, 2014), pp. 9, 79–80, 104. In fact, investment in IT has fallen off considerably since 2000.

3 Robert Solow, "We'd Better Watch Out," *New York Times Book Review*, July 12, 1987, p. 36.

4 The parameters of the law have shifted since its formulation.

5 Brynjolfsson and McAfee, *The Second Machine Age*, p. 106.

6 Paul A. David, "The Dynamo and the Computer: An Historical Perspective on the Modern Productivity Paradox," *American Economic Review*, LXXX/2 (January 1990), p. 355. Recently, in 2013, Paul Krugman invoked this famous essay in "The Dynamo and Big Data," published on his blog at https://krugman.blogs.nytimes.com, August 18, 2013.

7 David, "The Dynamo and the Computer," p. 359.

8 At the turn of the century, only 3 percent of American homes were powered by electricity.

9 David, "The Dynamo and the Computer," p. 356.

10 Ibid., p. 357.

11 Giovanni Arrighi argues, contrary to David Landes's canonical account of the first great depression, that "in reality, the economic system was not 'running down.' Production and investment continued to grow not just in the newly industrializing countries of the time (most notably, Germany and the U.S.) but in Britain as well." See "The Social and Political Hegemony of Global Turbulence," *New Left Review*, XX (March–April 2003), p. 5.

12 Paul Mason, *Postcapitalism: A Guide to Our Future* (London, 2015), p. 70.

13 John Lewis, "Bitesize: The Past Decade's Productivity Growth in Historical Context," Bank Underground, April 25, 2018; https://bankunderground.co.uk.

14 Mason, *Postcapitalism*, pp. xiii, 7.

15 Ibid., p. 144. My italics.
16 Robert Gordon's recent *The Rise and Fall of American Growth: The U.S. Standard of Living since the Civil War* (Princeton, NJ, 2016), makes an argument along the lines I've here proposed, and to which I am indebted.
17 Nick Srinicek's cogent *Platform Capitalism* (Cambridge, 2016) makes this important point.
18 That ride-sharing platforms like Uber and Lyft are highly unprofitable, if emblematic, boondoggles has been amusingly scrutinized for years by Izabella Kaminska on the *Financial Times*'s Alphaville blog: "The Taxi Unicorn's New Clothes," December 1, 2016; https://ftalphaville.ft.com.
19 Gordon, *The Rise and Fall of American Growth*, p. 587.
20 J. W. Mason, "What Recovery? The Case for Continued Expansionary Policy at the Fed," Roosevelt Institute, July 25, 2017, p. 51.; http://rooseveltinstitute.org.
21 Ibid., pp. 51–2.
22 Kenneth Rogoff, "Big Tech Is a Big Problem," Project Syndicate, July 2, 2018; www.project-syndicate.org.
23 As of July 2018.
24 Matthew Hunter, "Apple's Cash Pile Hits $285.1 billion, a Record," CNBC, February 1, 2018; www.cnbc.com.
25 Alex Shepherd, "Apple's Stock Market Scam," *New Republic*, August 3, 2018; https://newrepublic.com.
26 "Clouds Darken Trump's Sunny Economic View," *New York Times*, August 6, 2018, A20; my emphasis, www.nytimes.com.
27 Steve Pearlstein, "Beware the 'Mother of All Credit Bubbles'," *Washington Post*, June 8, 2018; www.washingtonpost.com.
28 This is a contrived term of business journalism to allow "consumer discretion" firms like Amazon and Netflix which operate primarily online services to be grouped under the rubric of "tech" stocks.
29 Ryan Vlastelica, "Stock Gains in 2018 Aren't Just a Tech Story, but They're Mostly a Tech Story," *MarketWatch*, July 12, 2018; www.marketwatch.com. "Amazon by itself accounts for more than a third – 35% – of the S&P 500's year-to-date return. Netflix accounts for 21% of the S&P's advance, while Microsoft and Apple together account for 27%."
30 "Too Much of a Good Thing," *The Economist*, March 26, 2016; www.economist.com.
31 Muge Adalet McGowan, Dan Andrews, and Valentine Millot, "The Walking Dead? Zombie Firms and Productivity Performance in OECD Countries," OECD Economics Department Working Paper 1372 (2017); cf. also Tim Harford, "Zombie Companies Walk among Us," *Financial Times*, February 22, 2018; www.ft.com.
32 Dan McCrum, "Rise of the Zombie Firm," *Financial Times*' Alphaville blog, March 1, 2018; https://ftalphaville.ft.com.

3 Army of Shadows

1 John Lewis, "Bitesize: The Past Decade's Productivity Growth in Historical Context," Bank Underground, April 25, 2018; https://bankunderground.co.uk; see also Jill Ward, "Britain's Trickiest Economic Challenge Is Back in the Spotlight," Bloomberg, July 1, 2018, who likewise describes this declining productivity growth as the "worst since 1794"; www.bloomberg.com.

2 The print version of the New York Times ran the story under the headline, "How Good? Words Fail Us," New York Times, June 1, 2018, A16, www.nytimes.com.

3 "Real Earnings News Release," Bureau of Labor Statistics, June 12, 2018; www.bls.gov.

4 Jeff Stein and Andrew Van Dam, "For the Biggest Group of American Workers, Wages Aren't Just Flat. They're Falling," Washington Post, June 15, 2018; www.washingtonpost.com. The article speculates that rising energy costs, due to a spike in the price of oil, accounted for the fall in purchasing power: workers drive to work, and heat their houses. Oil prices, fluctuating according to pressures that are often non-economic, are often evoked as external "shocks" to explain economic patterns that frustrate prevailing assumptions.

5 Lawrence Mishel and Heidi Shierholz, "A Decade of Flat Wages: The Key Barrier to Shared Prosperity and a Rising Middle Class," Economic Policy Institute, August 21, 2013; www.epi.org.

6 These numbers and projections can be found at www.bls.gov, accessed February 25, 2020.

7 "Civilian noninstitutional population" is defined by the Bureau of Labor Statistics as including all "persons 16 years of age and older residing in the 50 states and the District of Columbia who do not live in institutions (for example, correctional facilities, long-term care hospitals, and nursing homes) and who are not on active duty in the Armed Forces."

8 "America's 'Jobs for the Boys' Is Just Half the Employment Story," Financial Times (February 7, 2017); my italics. I thank William Clare Roberts for this reference.

9 On rising disability claims and payments, and their effect on questions of employment and wages, see the series of papers written by David Autor (singly or with colleagues), found here: https://economics. mit.edu/faculty/dautor/policy. For a journalistic account of the role played by disability payments and the stigma attached to them in the U.S., see Terrence McCoy's "Disabled and Disdained," Washington Post, June 21, 2018; www.washingtonpost.com; "Most people aren't employed when they apply for disability—one reason applicant rates skyrocketed during the recession. Full-time employment would, in fact, disqualify most applicants. And once on it, few ever get off, their

ranks uncounted in the national unemployment rate, which doesn't
include people on disability."

10 Nicholas Eberstadt, "Our Miserable 21st Century," *Commentary*
    (February 2017); www.commentarymagazine.com. In late 2016,
    Eberstadt published a book-length treatment of these matters:
    Men without Work: America's Invisible Crisis (West Conshohocken,
    PA, 2016). While Eberstadt's reactionary focus is on the purported
    erosion of patriarchal authority in the family, the *Financial Times*
    article cited above, and published in February 2017 as well, notes
    that for all the rhetoric of "missing men" that dominates discussions
    of contemporary worklessness, the dropout rate for American
    women (unlike other OECD countries) is climbing too.

11 "Solving the Productivity Puzzle: The Role of Demand and the
    Promise of Digitization," McKinsey Institute (February 2018);
    www.mckinsey.com.

12 "Private Non-farm Business Sector: Labor Productivity";
    https://fred.stlouisfed.org, accessed March 3, 2020.

13 U.S. Bureau of Labor Statistics, Manufacturing Sector: Labor
    Productivity [MPU9900063], retrieved from FRED, Federal Reserve
    Bank of St. Louis; https://fred.stlouisfed.org/series/MPU9900063,
    December 14, 2018.

14 Aaron E. Cobet and Gregory E. Wilson, "Comparing 50 Years of
    Labor Productivity in U.S. and Foreign Manufacturing," *Monthly
    Labor Review* (June 2002), pp. 51–65; www.bls.gov.

15 "Doing Less with More," *The Economist*, March 19, 2016;
    www.economist.com.

16 Howard Davies, "Why Is Productivity So Low since the Crisis –
    Particularly in the UK?," *The Guardian*, June 21, 2017;
    www.theguardian.com.

17 "Estimating the U.S. Labor Share," *Monthly Labor Review*, February
    2017; www.bls.gov.

18 Anwar Shaikh, *Capitalism: Competition, Conflict, Crises* (Oxford, 2016),
    p. 60; my emphasis.

19 Ibid., pp. 734ff.

20 Ibid., pp. 60, 72; my emphasis.

21 See, for example, "Labor Share of Output Has Declined since 1947,"
    March 7, 2017; www.bls.gov.

4 Approaching Zero

1 William J. Baumol, "Macroeconomics of Unbalanced Growth: Anatomy
   of the Urban Crisis," *American Economic Review*, LVII/3 (June 1967), p. 419.

2 "Share of Employment in Professional and Business Services at
   All-time High of 14 Percent in 2017," TED: The Economics Daily,
   Bureau of Labor Statistics, August 30, 2018; www.bls.gov.

3 Adam Smith, *An Inquiry into the Nature and Causes of the Wealth of Nations*, ed. Edwin Cannan (Chicago, IL: University of Chicago Press, 1976), p. 352.

4 An interesting case is the installation of dental crowns: these objects are today produced using sophisticated CNC machines, yet each crown is a unique object, fitted directly to the patient's tooth.

5 See Richard Walker, "Is There a Service Economy? The Changing Capitalist Division of Labor," *Science and Society*, XLIX/1 (Spring 1985), pp. 42–83.

6 In the following chapter, I discuss the intensification of the labor process through new, often digitally enhanced techniques of surveillance in the workplace.

7 Chapter Six of John Smith's *Imperialism in the Twenty-first Century: Globalization, Super-exploitation, and Capitalism's Final Crisis* (New York, 2016) offers a lucid examination of some of the contradictions I am tracking here.

8 Andrew Haldane and Vasileios Madouros, "What Is the Contribution of the Financial Sector?," Voxeu, November 22, 2011; https://voxeu.org.

9 Adair Turner, "The Zero-sum Economy," Institute for New Economic Thinking, August 20, 2018; www.ineteconomics.org.

10 "Do Alternative Measures of GDP Affect Its Interpretation?," *Current Issues in Economics and Finance*, XV/7 (November 2009); www.newyorkfed.org.

5 Circulation and Control

1 Luke A. Steward and Robert D. Atkinson, "The Greater Stagnation: The Decline in Capital Investment Is the Real Threat to U.S. Economic Growth," Information Technology and Innovation Foundation, October 2013; www2.itif.org.

2 In *The Rise and Fall of American Growth: The U.S. Standard of Living since the Civil War* (Princeton, NJ, 2016), Robert Gordon suggestively argues that these innovations, and the 1990s bump in growth they occasioned, represent the "climax" of a process of computerization beginning in the 1960s, rather than the opening of a new secular trend of economic transformation and dynamism.

3 On the role of the rate of profit on business investment and as the driving force shaping business cycles, see José A. Tapia's "Profits Encourage Investment, Investment Dampens Profits, Government Spending Does Not Prime the Pump: A DAG Investigation of Business-cycle Dynamics," May 2015; https://mpra.ub.uni-muenchen.de.

4 On this question, see Paul Mattick's *Theory as Critique: Essays on Capital* (Leiden, 2018). For a classic discussion of problems with profit statistics, see Oskar Morgenstern, *On the Accuracy of Economic Observations* (Princeton, NJ, 1965).

5 Bourgeois economics assumes that each of the "factors" consumed in production activities—land, machinery, and labor—contributes to the production of value, such that the distribution of revenues to landowners, entrepreneurs, and workers reflects these contributions.

6 By rising technical composition, Marx means an increase in the "amount" of machinery a single worker commands and valorizes. Here, we must think of both the size and scale of machinery: Marx has in mind the transition from small, handheld tools to large, complex machinery that raises labor productivity, understood in *physical* or technical-material terms. These are very approximate notions. By value composition, Marx means the value ratio of the two components of capital, constant and variable. In the example I give, cheaper machinery means the technical ratio of machines to workers will increase more quickly than the "value" composition.

7 Capitalist enterprises are fundamentally concerned not with labor productivity per se—output divided by labor *time*—but with output divided by labor costs: unit labor costs. This means that a business can raise "productivity," understood in this sense, without investing in new technologies.

8 Karl Marx, *Capital: A Critique of Political Economy*, vol. III, trans. David Fernach (London, 1991), p. 507.

9 Paul Mattick, *Marxism: The Last Refuge of the Bourgeoisie?* (Talgarth, 1983), p. 117. My emphasis.

10 This spatial dispersion, and the prevalence of smaller workplaces in the sphere of distribution, will have important implications for the workers who carry out these activities: these apparently structural features of the distribution process will pose significant obstacles to organizing these workers on sectoral and class lines. See my concluding chapter.

11 Fred Moseley, "The Rate of Profit and the Future of Capitalism," *Review of Radical Political Economics*, XXIX/4 (1997), pp. 23–41.

12 Ibid., p. 36.

13 I leave aside here the details of the debate whether "transportation" services are or are not productive of value in Marx's sense. Evidence for both positions is present in Marx's elliptical accounts.

14 Moseley, "Rate of Profit and the Future of Capitalism," p. 29. My emphasis.

15 Ibid., p. 36.

16 Kim Moody, *On New Terrain: How Capital Is Reshaping the Battlefield of Class War* (Haymarket, 2017), p. 75.

17 "The idea of wearing a monitoring bracelet evokes a modicum of creepiness, akin to the idea of wearing an ankle bracelet during house arrest," Alan Boyle, "Amazon Wins a Pair of Patents for Wireless Wristbands That Track Warehouse Workers," www.geekwire.com,

January 30, 2018; similar devices—"picking" technology—are being pioneered by the Knapps logistics firm in Germany.

18 "Inside China's Surveillance State," July 19, 2018, www.ft.com.

6 The Servant Economy

1 Between September 1982 and June 1983, the unemployment rate hovered between 10.1 and 10.8 percent.

2 "Occupations with the Largest Job Growth, 2004–14," TED: The Economics Daily, December 22, 2005; www.bls.gov.

3 Neema Ahmed, "Most Jobs Created since the Recession Have Been Low-paying," Axios, September 7, 2018, www.axios.com.

4 This job description is ubiquitous in employment ads for personal care aides.

5 And 5 percent in 1960. As of 2019, the projected expenditure is roughly 18 percent; it is less than 12 percent on average in other high-income countries.

6 By "grow most quickly" we mean not the rate of growth, but the absolute number of jobs.

7 U.S. Bureau of Labor Statistics, "Economic Projections: 2014–24 News Release," December 8, 2015, www.bls.gov.

8 David Autor and David Dorn, "The Growth of Low Skill Service Jobs and the Polarization of the U.S. Labor Market," *American Economic Review*, CIII/5 (2013), pp. 1553–97.

9 This was especially pronounced in the early to mid-twentieth century in the case of "domestic labor," as washing machines and dishwashers became available even to working-class families in rich countries.

10 David H. Autor, "Why Are There Still So Many Jobs? The History and Future of Workplace Automation," *Journal of Economic Perspectives*, XXIX/3 (Summer 2015), p. 17.

11 The primary driver is always production cost per unit, since individual capitals are concerned above all with producing a given unit of some good or service more cheaply than competing firms; whether they arrive at these lower production costs by means of lower labor costs or by some other means is a secondary question. In many cases, firms that have dramatically cheaper labor inputs can compete with highly capitalized firms with higher labor costs.

12 "Skilled" labor is often a category that sticks to those craft traditions that are particularly well organized and are able both to control access to a particular segment of the job market (via guilds, unions, and so on) and to resist or forestall their own replacement by a new division of labor, a new labor process, and the introduction of "de-skilling" machinery.

13 Autor and Dorn, "The Growth of Low Skill Service Jobs and the Polarization of the u.s. Labor Market," *American Economic Review*, CIII/5 (2013):1555n3.

14 "The Sick Man of the Euro," *The Economist*, June 3, 1999; www.economist.com, accessed October 29, 2019.

15 Katinka Barysch, "Germany: The Sick Man of Europe?"; Center for European Reform policy brief, www.cer.eu, December 2003.

16 Olivier Cyran, "Germany's Working Poor," *The Nation*, September 6, 2017, www.thenation.com; my italics.

17 Ibid.

18 "How to Keep Populists Small and Marginal," *The Economist*, October 15, 2010, www.economist.com. It is arguable that the source of Germany's economic "boom" has been lower unit costs of labor, not higher productivity. After all, more labor in low-productivity occupations would draw down the aggregate productivity of German workers.

19 Christian Odendahl, "Germany after the Hartz Reforms: Can the spd Protect German Labor?," *Foreign Affairs*, September 11, 2017, www.cer.eu.

7 An Absolute Law

1 *Capital: A Critique of Political Economy*, vol. i, trans. Ben Fowkes (London, 1976), p. 492.

2 Ibid., p. 517.

3 Ibid. Translation modified; my italics.

4 Marx, *Capital*, vol. i, p. 570.

5 Ibid., p. 574.

6 Kim Moody, "u.s. Labor: What's New, What's Not?," *Solidarity*, May 1, 2016.

7 It is sufficient to note that the ratio of non-residential fixed investment to GDP hit its postwar peak in the first quarter of 1982, during which GDP dropped by almost 2 percent.

8 Robert Rowthorn and Ramana Ramaswamy, "Deindustrialization: Its Causes and Implications," IMF Working Paper, April 1997, p. 22.

9 James Boggs, *The American Revolution: Pages from a Negro Worker's Notebook* (New York, 1963), p. 44.

10 Beverly Silver, *Forces of Labor: Workers' Movements and Globalization since 1870* (Cambridge, 2003), pp. 113–22, 172.

11 Ibid., p. 118.

12 Boggs, *The American Revolution*, p. 52.

Acknowledgments

The ideas presented in this book took shape through conversations with many friends, and over many years. It is impossible to name all to whom I owe an often sizable debt. Should they read these pages, they will recognize their contributions.

It is an honor to publish these ideas with Reaktion Books. I want, in particular, to thank Vivian Constantinopoulos for her interest in publishing it as well as her editorial acumen and patience. Amy Salter has ably shepherded the book through production during a particularly trying moment with care and precision.

I owe a special debt to Paul Mattick, who has been a friend and mentor for some years now. I would not have written this book without his interest and encouragement. He has suggested, inspired and meticulously edited much of what I have written in recent years, and I hope that, at crucial moments in this book, his contribution to my thinking is clear to all.

My wife and son, Rachel and Remy, have supported this project through its ups and downs. They are my two closest friends, and I would not have it any other way.